# The Noble Generation

*edited by*

Stephen F. Neubauer
Joan R. Neubauer

*Andy,*

*Best wishes for all your tomorrows.*

*Joan R. Neubauer*

*Steve Neubauer*

P.O. Box 1785
Georgetown, TX 78627
http://www.WordWright.biz

Printed in the United States of America

*Dedicated to every generation
that strives to find
its own nobility.*

# *Table of Contents*

# *Preface*

The book you hold in your hands, *The Noble Generation*, is a direct outgrowth of Noble Ambassadors, a senior outreach program, which began as a joint project of the Texas Department on Aging and Barnes & Noble Booksellers in Austin, Texas. The program, which began in 2000, was designed to reach out to senior citizens by presenting monthly programs of interest at each area Barnes & Noble store.

A variety of people spoke on a number of topics over a period of several months. However, it very quickly became clear that people showed the most interest in writing and telling their own stories for their children, grandchildren and future generations.

Over time, the monthly meetings focused on writing personal stories for the book. Authors and others from the community generously volunteered their time and talents to guide and encourage the many participants. And they all had wonderful stories to tell. Thus was born *The Noble Generation*, a book written entirely by Central Texas Seniors. We hope you find these stories as enjoyable to read as we have and that they will inspire you to write your own.

This book, born of community involvement, will provide help and support to the community. All profits from the sale of this book will be donated to Literacy Austin. So we encourage you to purchase several copies for family and friends.

Barnes & Noble would like to thank Ken Bomar and Russell Smith of the Texas Department on Aging who helped spread the word and the enthusiasm about this project. We also must acknowledge the enormous efforts of Joan and Steve Neubauer who served as both editors and tireless promoters of this book. Finally, and most importantly, we must recognize all of the many men and women who contributed their stories. This truly is their book. They truly are *The Noble Generation*.


Jeff Burandt
Frank Campbell
Colleen Devine
Stephanie Nelson
Angela Perez
Jo Virgil
Barnes & Noble
Community Relations Managers

# *Introduction*

Family lore has a way of capturing the imagination. We all love to hear how our parents, grandparents, aunts and uncles coped with problems growing up. We giggle with the knowledge that those revered elders managed to get into scrapes with their parents just like we did. And we look at our parents in a very different way when we find out they served time in the corner for sliding down the banister at school. Every family has those stories, and we pass them down from generation to generation.

This particular generation, this Noble Generation that is still with us, has had a rough row to hoe. They have suffered through The Great Depression, served their country in World War II, and endured the Cold War. Yet, they emerged with the strength of tempered steel and hearts of gold. They have given birth to us, and tried to give us all they had found lacking in their lives.

Their greatest gift has been their lives and the stories they told from the heart. When we were children, we listened to their stories of bread lines and sad good-byes as brothers and sons and husbands headed out to fight a war. As children, we had little appreciation for what they did. As adults, however, we have come to a new understanding of their efforts, their successes, and yes, even their failures.

The stories within this book all come from family lore. They are very personal stories, each told with a unique voice. To maintain the voice of every author, we have kept editing to a minimum, so while you may see a different turn of phrase, or a word you haven't seen used in years, revel in the unique quality of every author's work. Read their story and put yourself in their shoes. Ask yourself how you would feel; how you would react; and how it would change you.

The stories themselves will make you laugh and cry and reflect upon the tales your own family has told. They will give you a new appreciation for this generation that has paved the way for us. They will make you want to say thank you to those who have taken up the challenges and emerged triumphant. Today, we live in freedom because of them.

To you, *The Noble Generation*, we say thank you.


Sincerely,
The Editors

Stephen F. Neubauer
Joan R. Neubauer

# Acknowledgements

*The Noble Generation* was a fun project to work on, but we could not have done it alone. The editors wish to thank the many who helped in a variety of ways to produce this book.

First, our thanks go out to Cathy Lane and Linda Germain of Barnes & Noble and Ken Bomar and Russell Smith of the Texas Department on Aging for the idea. Their desire to reach out into the community gave birth to an idea that has borne sweet fruit.

Second, we'd like to thank the community relations managers at all the Austin area Barnes & Noble stores for inviting us into their stores to tell people about the project and encourage them to submit their stories. They spent many hours talking with people, explaining the project and logging in the many manuscripts that people submitted. Thank you Jeff Burandt, Frank Campbell, Colleen Devine, Angela Perez, and Jo Virgil.

Without volunteers to type, mentor and proof the manuscript, we would have found this an impossible task. We owe much gratitude to our volunteers: Bettye Baldwin, Ray Bronk, Sarah Bryce, Joan Hall, Mary Hobbs, Janet Kilgore, Carol Menchu, Elenor Neubauer, Ellice Smart, Lois Strout, Sue Tome, June Venable, Artie Stockton, Herbert Teat, Diana Urban, and Cindy Wiegand.

Our thanks also goes out to the senior program and retirement home directors who invited us to tell their members and residents about this project. Their help and encouragement aided us immensely in securing submissions.

We also wish to acknowledge the writers, many of them part of the StoryCircle Network, who submitted material for this project. Some contributors sent multiple articles. We regret, however, that we could not include all of them. We found them all wonderful, but because of space limitations, were forced to choose.

We would like to say thank you to the following writers of memorable stories: Kaye Voigt Abikhaled, Jane C. Accord, Nadene Walker Anderson, Paula Stephens Bishop, Ruby Bishop, Linda M. Bonner, A. F. Borello, Ken Braselton, Ray Bronk, Mary Bruce, Sarah Bryce, Cathryn Burdick, Esther Hughes Burns, Roger M. Busfield, Jr., Barbara Carr, Jerry Carson, Judy Crawford, Penelope Dale, Lita De Los Santos, Glenn Dehlin, Joyce A. Dehlin, Carin Eagleston, Lois Earley, Mary Katherine Earney, Michael Egbert, Trudie M. Eklund, Fredie Eklund, Rizer Everett, Patricia Riggs Flathouse, Judith S. Flournoy, Ellen Lange Foster, Dora T. Frost, Shirley Gaines, Faye Gish, Joy H. Goodale, Elsa G. Goodson, Mr. Graham, Maudi Greenwood, Sam Hahs, Mary Lee Harris, Stacey Hasbrook, Roy A. Henley, Karen Hett, Mary Reece Hobbs, Ann Holden, Joan Tessier Hollier, Robert Hunt, Angela Irvine, Legia Palacios Jimenez, Joyce Carson Joiner, Molly Juvenal, Mary P. Kann, Janie Kirkpatrick, Carolyn Knutsen, Zella A. Landfair, Ruth Lehman, Deanna Johnson Lockett, P. Paulette MacDougal, Barbara Busch Markeson, Wayne Meredith Miller, Mauri Molina, Rosemarie Mueller, Peter Munk, Helen Nardecchia, Ruth Niedermeier, Martin E. Parker, Dorothy Patton, Alexander Paxson, Jane Peppard, Jo Ann Peveto, Jim Remmert, Donna Van Stratten Remmert, Linda Reynolds, Melvin C. Roach, Max B. Scheider, Carolyn J. Scheider, Zella Shaper, Dorothy Shepard, Ellice Smart, Irene Chute Smith, Mary Gordon Spence, Dorine Stewart, Lois Taylor, Herbert Teat, June Venable, John Venable,

Ginnie Voelker, Linda M.Watkins, Trudy Wheeler, Anne Zesiger, and Suzanne Vance Zoch.

Finally, we apologize in advance if we have forgotten to include anyone in these acknowledgements who have given their time and talents for this project. We assure you it was purely an oversight.

We thank every one of you for all that you have done. We hope that you will share our pride in this book and say, "This book is part of me."

# America's Noble Legacy

## Jim Remmert

Like most Americans, I love our country and when I attend an event where they play the "Star Spangled Banner," my emotions frequently get the better of me. I am not emotional because of what goes on in Washington, D.C, the state capitol or City Hall. The National Anthem causes me to reminisce about all the ordinary Americans who, for more than two hundred years, have given so much of themselves in the unselfish defense of freedom and support of their fellow man. In my lifetime, ordinary Americans who have little political or economic power have gone off to World War II, the Korean War, the Vietnam War and the Persian Gulf War. I think of these men and women when I hear the National Anthem.

I also wonder who among the men and women I served with in the Second Infantry Division did not return from Vietnam. My thoughts also fix on my next-door neighbor who was a foot soldier in the Korean War and who at age sixty-nine still attends Third Army reunions.

I'm also thinking of the many acts of self-sacrifice and heroism in this country that have come to light and the many more that haven't. I'm thinking of all the people who have volunteered as missionaries, to help people in Third World countries. I'm thinking of all the people who took a stand for equality during the civil rights movement. I'm thinking of all the people in this country who volunteer to help others in need. In short, my thoughts are of all the wonderful, unselfish people who make a community of this piece of geography that we call the United States of America.

The outpouring of charity, volunteerism and self-sacrifice in the aftermath of the September 11, 2001 terrorist attacks is a more recent example of Americanism. New Yorkers closed their businesses to volunteer their services and that of their employees, in the rescue efforts. On the day of the attacks, police officers and fire fighters ignored their natural instincts of self-preservation and ran toward the obvious danger to rescue others who could not help themselves. People from as far away as Texas and California dropped what they did for a living and traveled to New York or Washington to volunteer their help. The American people contributed over $1 billion to help family survivors get through the ordeal of September 11, 2001 and get back on their feet. This help poured out as naturally as if the people affected were next-door neighbors.

One man explained in an interview why he closed down his business, drove 800 miles, and volunteered to help in the rescue effort for over a month. He said that he felt compelled to help because the victims and their families needed it. If he and his family were the victims, he knew they'd help him.

He said, "We're Americans and in America we help each other when it's needed."

When I hear the "Star Spangled Banner" or "God Bless America," I think of these people and I am moved by the fact that it goes with being an American to assist others in need. What makes our country great is not its government or its political leaders but our country's people and the values for which they stand. Americans have different races, religions, and ethnic backgrounds. However, we share values first expressed in the Declaration of Independence and the Constitution. Over the last two hundred years, other values have evolved and become a part of our culture.

Examples include our tradition of patriotism, our recognition of achievement, our respect for work, our religious belief, diversity and tolerance, our veneration of family, our tradition of entrepreneurial capitalism, our admiration for individualism, our tradition of peaceful dissent and our heritage of contributing to causes larger than ourselves. Our families, churches and schools pass these traditions from generation to generation and they comprise a big part of the glue that holds our society together. In the absence of our shared values, we'd be little more than a shifting coalition of interest groups bound together by mutual convenience.

My twenty years of traveling and living outside the United States has convinced me that our country really is different from others. It is diverse in culture, race and ethnicity. This diversity is one of our strengths. Our culture has imported and incorporated into itself the language, customs, food, traditions, technology, and crafts of almost every other culture in the world. We also have our own collective culture that is unique and distinct from any other culture in the world. We eat moo-shu pork, chicken cacciatore, tempura, and tacos but we also like hot dogs, buffalo chicken wings and Philadelphia cheese steaks.

We are simultaneously the product of those countries from whence our ancestors came and a culture distinct from any other in the world. Americans are optimistic, entrepreneurial and we are not afraid of taking risks. We have a sense of purpose and a sense of humor. We are a self-confident people. We think that we can go to the moon and we have the ability to marshal the national will to do it. Americans have a tradition of commitment to causes greater than themselves.

Americans are a generous people. Annual contributions by Americans to private charities exceed $120 billion. American religious organizations provide teachers and social workers throughout the world. Americans volunteer their time and work for every conceivable charitable purpose: schools, soup kitchens, fire fighting, housing for the poor, libraries, cultural organizations, substance abuse counseling, secondhand clothing stores for the poor, coaching youth sports, religious organizations, etc.

Religion has been a significant source of moral standards, benevolence and social organization in America. In the 1960s, religious organizations led the civil rights movement and its effort to end discrimination, establish equality for all under the law and affirm the principle of merit as the basis for reward in the United States. A minister, Dr. Martin Luther King, led the movement and articulated the goal better than anyone else. In his "I Have a Dream" speech, he said that his dream for America was for a society in which the content of one's character, not the color of one's skin, would determine each person's worth.

Some of the cultures from which our ancestors immigrated have a tradition that gives position, birthright and status a place in an individual's opportunities in life. Our country rejected that kind of caste society. In 1835 Alexis De Tocqueville, a Frenchman who was then touring the United States, wrote a collection of essays called *On Democracy in America.* His essays are often referred to as the most insightful observations ever written about our society. One of his observations was that we Americans are particularly adept at forming associations outside of government to accomplish shared objectives.

What De Tocqueville said in 1835 is as true today as it was then. We Americans have a great facility for identifying common denominators between each other and affiliating with each other for a common purpose. We assemble in private groups for almost every conceivable purpose; social, civic, charitable, hobby, political, sports, business and religious. The Internet now facilitates our ability to associate with others for common purposes. Americans have an extraordinary ability to voluntarily come together that reminds us of our beginnings as a nation.

The signers of the Declaration of Independence came together to declare their independence from the King of Great Britain and to secure their inalienable right to "Life, Liberty and the pursuit of Happiness." Their words led to the Revolutionary War and began the long line of ordinary Americans who, as written in the last line of the Declaration of Independence, "—mutually pledge to each other our Lives, our Fortunes and our sacred Honor."

This commitment of the American people to each other and to freedom is America's noble legacy that I proudly pass from my generation to that of my children.

# *Indian Summer Memory*

### Barbara Carr

Touching a treasured fossil rock, I remember the time
my family followed our Father up a winding trail
along one overgrown Cherokee trail by an ancient
creek bed, explored our ancestry near
Tahlequah, Oklahoma.
With thick layers of fresh fall leaves underfoot
and forest smells of life and decay in our nostrils,
crisp air cleared minds, nipped faces and hands.
Near the top of the bluff, a clear mountain spring
bubbled out of the ground.
We made hand-cups and tasted its sweet water,
sipped it while we looked down in the valley
at the farm in Peavine Hollow where Father
had grown up.
He picked up a large stone full of fossils on the edge
of the spring, a stone rough on one side, water-smoothed
on the other.
Dozens of shells and tiny skeleton formations, mingled
together in death, decorated that unique rock.
Father entrusted it to me to carry for the rest
of our adventure.
That one perfect Indian Summer day,
spent with my family, merged with the fossils
on the stone and became a part of my life.
Today I stroke the fossil stone . . .
and remember.

# A Father's Moral on Life

Stacey Hasbrook

Dad didn't talk about that time much, those teenage years just after he became an orphan and lived precariously on the streets of San Antonio, Texas. In 1939 his father, a well-known building contractor, suddenly died, the victim of a hit-and-run taxi when Dad was twelve. The very next year, according to what he and his brother Sam remembered, their beloved mother willed herself to death from grief. At thirteen, the age of an average seventh grader, James Richard Hasbrook, the youngest of five children, suddenly found himself homeless.

I asked him once why he hadn't gone to live with a sibling. He explained that the three oldest had already married and lived quite a distance away. He didn't have the money for a bus ticket or a phone call. He thought they were too poor to help, but I think perhaps pride prevented his asking. Sam, the next to the youngest and Dad's closest companion, found a temporary home with the family of a school friend, leaving Dad totally alone and penniless.

That would have been the end of the story as I knew it except for one afternoon, when my father heard my young daughter complaining about not having the toys she wanted.

Pop, the grandchildren called him, gently took her up

onto his lap, rocked back and forth, and calmly stated, "Did you know when your mother was little, we were very poor, and she had to make all of her toys herself?"

Her eyes grew large and round, and she glanced at me nervously, but he kept rocking. Then he went on to tell her about his youth, and for the first time, I learned of the details that made this man the loving, protective father that I knew.

He calmly explained that he had struggled with having only one set of clothes and the overwhelming embarrassment of being so dirty he could not find a job to buy food, much less go to school. He told of the kind waitress who allowed him to come into a tiny cafe and sit at the end of the counter to get out of the bad weather. She would bring him cups of hot water in which he mixed ketchup, salt, and pepper to fill his aching stomach with a weak substitute for tomato soup. She even began slipping him crackers and sometimes leftovers when she could.

I don't know how long he had suffered this way or if he had ever known her name. But as he rocked my child back and forth, I silently sent up a prayer of thanks for this kind woman who must have been heartbroken to see such a handsome young boy wasting away before her eyes.

Eventually this same woman told him about a connection at the YMCA, and how he and Sam could qualify to move in. She had spent a great deal of time and effort finding a solution for someone she really didn't know. She had looked past the dirt and pain to see a young boy in need of divine intervention.

Dad glowed as he recalled the lukewarm shower that rinsed away the layers of dirt and the smooth softness of the mattress bare of any linens. There was nothing in his room but that bed and an empty dresser. He remembered writing in a notebook at night to cope with losing the familiar world he had known and to give thanks for the blessings that had saved his life. He missed his mother most. I would give anything to have that journal now, but he said he had lost it somewhere along the line. I often wonder if he merely threw it with its painful memories away when his life changed for the better.

It was at the YMCA that Dad's fate began, as he said, "to turn to gold." He soon had a job that barely made ends meet, but brought his spirit back. He had a few more clothes, including a warm coat, and could afford to eat. Sadly, he could not return to the athletic competition he had once loved at school, but he worked out with the weights in the gym at the Y to get back in shape. Before long, he was once again a handsome young man.

One day after school and before he had to go to work, he happened to see a play rehearsal at the Y, and on the stage, the most beautiful girl he had ever seen. That young girl eventually became his wife, and together they slowly built a successful life. In spite of everything, my dad finished high school and completed two years of college before setting his career path with civil service. I came along almost immediately during those difficult early years of their marriage thus his story of my toyless childhood.

When Pop hesitated as if determining where to end the story, my daughter jumped off his lap to chase after one of his cats. He and I remained in our chairs silently enjoying a moment of companionship, and for me, a revelation. I knew I had grown up very aware of the lack of money, but I had never thought of our family as poor. I don't know if my daughter learned a lesson on Pop's knee that day, but his eldest daughter found the true meaning of wealth, the kind that does not tarnish with time.

# A Maryland Childhood

## Trudy Wheeler

My father, John H. Williams, a veteran of World War I, secured employment with Civil Service and taught occupational therapy to shell-shocked veterans. In 1923, he transferred to Perry Point, Maryland, a government reservation where the veterans were warehoused, an ideal environment for two growing girls. My sister Lillian and I took every advantage offered.

The Perry family had owned the property for generations and made it a productive Maryland plantation. The land, situated on a peninsula, jutted out where the Susquehanna River and the Chesapeake Bay converged. The manor house, in which the manager of the Reservation lived, had a commanding view of the river. Age-old boxwood trees in its backyard were wonderful places to hide from the pirates coming up the Bay to capture us, or from Indians in their canoes poised for attack. An old, dilapidated gristmill at the edge of the river had ground corn for the Continental Army.

You entered the Reservation by turning off Route 40, the road connecting Philadelphia and Baltimore. Going through a tunnel under the Pennsylvania Railroad, you stopped at a gate. If the guards knew you, there was no trouble. The casual traveler did not get in. I remember a farmer coming in with his truck every week during the summer to sell produce. The egg-lady was another, so Mother always had fresh eggs for cooking.

After driving down a little hill, the village for the government employees began. It had an orderly appearance comprised of tree lined paved streets with curbs and sidewalks. "Doctors' Row" had bigger and finer houses with lovely views of the Susquehanna.

Situated two miles from the village, stood the extensive veterans hospital. The three-story dormitories had barred windows. Tennis courts, a golf course and a movie theater with bowling alleys in the basement, helped the veterans recover. Lillian and I went there only if accompanied by our father.

The school, a long white building at the opposite end of the village from the gate, contained eight grades. The classrooms and auditorium were located on both sides of a wide, wide hall. On rainy days, that hall was our playground. On its sides at intervals were signs, "A place for everything and everything in its place." To this day, I like an orderly house.

Churches weren't allowed on the reservation. However, my mother was one of the ringleaders who established a Sunday school held Sunday afternoons in the schoolhouse. I remember memorizing the books of the Bible. My teacher gave me a square, blue scarf, which I did not appreciate or use.

The Susquehanna dominated our lives, and was our playground, no matter there were cement sidewalks for roller-skating, and two tennis courts at our disposal. In the winter when freezing weather made the river a skating rink, we clamped ice skates on our shoes and skated on the thin ice formed over the mud flats. We spent summer days canoeing, swimming, and diving for oyster shells. We claimed as our swimming hole the channel the government dug for the pipes carrying clear river water to the pumping station for the village and hospital.

That channel holds a terrifying memory for me. It was quite deep with only a foot or two around the edges for the non-swimmers. By the age of nine or ten, I was an experienced swimmer. One day, a big-boned, older girl slipped into deep water. I could see she was in trouble. I reached out a hand to pull her to safety. Instead, she jerked me to her and proceeded to climb on my shoulders. The watery gray light above my head did not cause me to panic. Fortunately, the girl's older brother was watching and saw us go under. He said later he didn't know he could swim that fast. He pulled us from the water. The ordeal sapped my energy but in a day or two, I was back swimming in the channel.

Our house was third from the gate. Built of white clapboard, it had three bedrooms and one bath. A full basement contained the furnace, coal bin, washing machine and old trunks. For our circumstances, our house was well furnished. Various pieces of rich cut glass were on display, the result of my father's being an incorporator and partner in the early 1900s in a cut glass factory in Philadelphia. In particular, one vase was always the focal point of our living room. We spoke of it in capital letters, FATHER'S VASE. If we ever broke it, Lillian and I knew to just start running; we no longer had a home.

One Sunday afternoon, after attending church and having

Sunday dinner, I started to play jacks on the porch. When Mother saw what I was doing, she stopped me. It was the Sabbath. I could read a book, study, or go for a walk, but I could not play games.

Often, the four of us went for rides on Sunday afternoons. Lillian and I in the backseat enjoyed seeing all the farms, woods and streams we passed. One Sunday Mother discovered we were near the egg-lady's house and suggested we stop there to buy eggs for next week's use. The egg-lady would not sell them. It was the Sabbath. She carried on no commerce on that day. Mother was chagrined. She should have known better.

We paid a nominal house rent and nothing for electricity or coal. When we needed coal, a truck pulled up to the side of the house, extended a long chute into a window of the cellar, and poured into the coal bin. We also used coal for the cooking range. Mother, married late in life, did not care to bake. She "did her duty" and turned out wholesome meals. When an electric stove replaced the old fashioned range, Mother never had quite the same touch.

Daddy was in charge of the furnace. During the winter months, he kept a fire going all the time. When it was time to go to bed, he "banked" it. In the morning, he stirred the embers and added coal. I remember eating breakfast in the kitchen many times while the house warmed up.

The grocery store, library, movie house, ice cream parlor and barber shop were located two blocks south of our home. No sedate walking for me, I'd leave the house at a run. When our grandfather bought a bike for Lillian and me, I leaped on it and pedaled away. I never remember her riding the bike we were supposed to share.

For their engagement, Daddy gave Mother a fine

diamond. In the summer of 1927, they pawned the diamond to pay for a trip.

On the back end of the Buick, Daddy built a big compartmentalized box from which Mother cooked. Along the left side of the car, he placed an expandable fence, making it necessary for everyone to enter and exit from the right side of the car. This fence held a tent that was attached to the car at night when we camped out. Mother and Daddy slept in it while Lillian and I slept in the car on a tarp that somehow fastened to the four corners of the interior.

We left home early one July morning, packed as expertly as only my Mother could. That night we camped behind a schoolhouse in Pennsylvania. Many nights on our journey, we stayed in Tourist Homes. These private homes, advertised by a sign on the front lawn, needed no reservations, and did not serve meals. Our destination was The Thousand Islands on the St. Lawrence River. We indulged in a boat ride around The Thousand Islands, which I recall vividly.

Being just a step from Canada, we drove across the border to Montreal where we stayed with a French family. Lillian and I could not understand a word, but we found it fascinating to hear French spoken.

Many road constructions were in progress and after passing a particularly difficult spot, we stopped to rest. Blackberries were growing across the ditch, which paralleled the road. In my mind's eye, I can still see the scene. Daddy jumped across the ditch. Hardly touching ground, he jumped back. A snake lay coiled beneath the berry bushes. He wanted no part of that snake.

Our trip was the highlight of my childhood. We visited other states and another country. We saw how other people lived, and tasted different foods. We saw mountains and tumbling streams. After two weeks, we returned home, a beautiful place to be.

Mother, during the following months, saved penny after penny. Finally, she redeemed her diamond. Our world was in order, but never the same. Our vision had expanded.

# Depression Days

## Mary Bruce

Though only five, I sensed the disintegration of my world. The people on my block had gathered in the street, in small, tight groups. No one laughed or spoke. I saw worried frowns and lowered heads and eyes filled with fear.

My best friend, the tomboy of the block, the one I had always admired because she could beat anyone, even the boys, in a marbles game, saw my confusion.

"All the banks closed. No one has any money." She shook her bag of marbles to underline the severity of the situation.

My faithful dog, Muggs, licked my hand.

"You dumb dog!" my friend said. "You don't even know the sky is falling!" she said with the assurance of the Queen of England.

I doubled my hands into fists, ready to defend my faithful friend. "He's *not* dumb!" I heard myself saying. "You're too dumb to know he's telling me he's sorry!" I felt better being unreasonable and taking out my frustrations on my best friend. She let me get by with it and hung her head to let me know she was sorry.

"Let's play marbles," she said, getting on more comfortable ground.

She headed for a big shade tree, bent down and drew a large circle in the sand with a twig.

"You first," she said generously.

The boys sidled in, still leery of playing with a Super Woman who had beaten them before.

I wasn't so wise. I went into the fray, headfirst with all the zeal of a five-year-old. I would win because the world was losing. I would show them all. I had a noble cause.

Muggs licked on my hand again to assure me I was king of the hill. Of course I lost. That's the day I left my childhood in the shifting sand.

# *The Great Depression*

## Trudie M. Eklund

I was just a child during the Great Depression but I remember hearing much about those worrisome times. My father worked for the Philadelphia Rapid Transit Company and while he was never completely out of a job, regular paydays were few and far between. One week he'd work only two days, another week, if he were lucky, three days. This schedule lasted until 1939 when Philadelphia's industrial base began humming again after President Roosevelt lifted the arms embargo against the Allies.

Though well-known as The City of Brotherly Love, Philadelphia is also known as A City of Homes. Unfortunately many families with no jobs and no paydays, lost their homes. It was unsettling to roam through the neighborhood and come face to face with foreclosure signs nailed to the front doors. Adults out for an evening stroll would make a game of counting the abandoned houses and compare their new total with the previous week's number. Unfortunately, every sign meant another family had no place to live.

We moved a lot during that time. If my father heard of cheaper rent a few blocks away, we'd pack our belongings.

One month we moved because the rent was $2.00 less than what we had been paying. When the depression deepened and job worries for our family mounted, he found a place a dollar cheaper and another time we relocated to a new address to save fifty cents.

For several months, we dared not unpack our meager belongings because we knew my father would find a cheaper house somewhere else. But still we felt fortunate, at least we had a roof over our heads and we still had a few dollars left from savings, withdrawn only a few days before the dreaded and all too familiar sign graced the neighborhood's bank window, "Closed by the Governor." It was little comfort when we learned in 1933 that over 5,000 banks in the country had failed.

The shelters filled rapidly. When we lived near one of the larger police stations in the Olney section of the city, every afternoon we'd watch a little group congregate outside the station's heavy metal doors. Men, with deep worry lines etched in their faces, in tattered and worn clothing and with nowhere else to go, shuffled slowly through the line, hoping to make it inside for a shower, a meal and a bed for the night. Churches served free breakfasts almost every day. They usually spent the rest of the day searching for work or begging.

During the latter part of the nineteenth century, most major cities could boast a large park, and Philadelphia was no exception. By the 1930s however, Fairmont Park had become more than just a pleasant place to stroll, play ball or picnic. Families lived there in crude shacks made from old wooden egg crates, uneven boards, or whatever else they could accumulate. They dubbed the shacks "Little Hoovervilles" in "honor" of President Herbert Hoover, whom they blamed for the country's dire economic conditions.

The shacks afforded little shelter during heavy rainstorms or the frosty East Coast winters. Winter, however, could be a mixed blessing. A heavy snow meant obtaining work shoveling the white stuff from the downtown sections of Broad, Market, Chestnut and Walnut Streets. A man considered himself fortunate if he received $2.00 from the city for his day of backbreaking labor. While many men stuck it out in Philadelphia, others fled to Pennsylvania's anthracite region. My father was especially despondent when he watched his favorite cousin pack and leave for a mining job upstate. Another relative rode the rails and made his way to California where he ended up picking figs for ten cents a box, and a box had to weigh in at fifty pounds. All of my father's relatives returned the year before the country entered World War II.

As the country's economy languished, we heard about the many groups protesting the hard times. In Bucks County, Pennsylvania (not far from Philadelphia's city limits), farmers organized and joined a countrywide organization to protest low prices for their crops. We worried how far the movement would go. When we heard several states follow suit it was no surprise to hear that all milk deliveries from Bucks County to Philadelphia would be curtailed or completely halted. Like so many neighborhood families, we didn't have much money for milk, so the movement caused little disruption to our lives.

From my front steps, I watched another phenomenon develop. During early spring afternoons, a small band of women would appear as if out of nowhere to roam up and down the neighborhood streets searching front yards for dandelions, which they carried home in old tattered muslin bags. Our family never ate dandelions. Instead, we "feasted" on oatmeal, sometimes for breakfast, dinner and supper. I grew to hate oatmeal and still do.

Rumors spread that women were also wandering around the busy docks near the Delaware River. Usually they remained well hidden until a piece of fruit or a few potatoes spilled from a crate. If they knew the right place to hide and if they were quick enough, their family would have some food that evening.

Life fell into set patterns. After breakfast, Mother would determine our ice needs for that day. In the summer, we usually needed fresh ice every other day for our three door wooden icebox. As the ice melted, the water dripped in a shallow pan on the floor under the box and we had to constantly empty it, hopefully without sloshing it all over the floor. Actually, the system was pretty ingenious.

To let the iceman know the size of ice we required that day, a large 16-inch square cardboard sign with figures on all four sides rested in the front window. The number 35 at the top meant we needed a sizable block of ice. For 25, the iceman hurried up the steps with a medium chunk of ice. If ten showed, then we needed a much smaller piece. We loved to see the iceman's truck making its way up the street.

During the warm months, the truck acted as a magnet drawing children from neighboring streets hoping to get a chunk or even a small sliver of ice that spilled onto the street as the iceman was chopping the customer's ice to specifications.

Few families could afford radios or telephones. When important events occurred around the country, the lucky family with the radio sent children to neighbors with the news. This is how we learned that President Franklin Roosevelt had been reelected in November 1936 which caused many heated arguments on neighborhood porches. It was how we learned of the worsening economy in mid-1937. Factories were announcing new layoffs and several Works Progress Administration (WPA) civil projects were cut. Many fathers and older brothers had found work clearing land, building bridges, hospitals, schools, and various other construction projects so the news caused deeper worry lines in the adults' faces.

We did without telephones because we had to, and we didn't feel deprived. Mail service was reasonably efficient and if we had the money for a two-cent stamp, we wrote a few pages every few weeks to our relatives in other parts of the city. On our street, only one family had a telephone and in the spirit of the times of hanging together, they gave out their phone number to be used in case of emergency. This was how we learned of my aunt's death in December of 1937.

Eventually our family's fortune took a turn for the better. The Philadelphia Navy Yard was retooling and it wasn't long before trains were making their way to and from the Naval base carrying workers grateful for steady work. When my father worked four days a week we ate better and by late 1939 he was overjoyed at his new forty-hour week schedule. If we had a dollar or two remaining after paying the bills, we tucked it safely into the cellar's rafters. My parents, no different from many Americans, had completely lost their faith in banks.

Little did we know that within two years we would be called on to live through more hardships and shortages. The world seemed to be tearing apart and soon we heard the dreaded words: A state of war now exists.

# Depression Days in Fort Worth

Roger M. Busfield, Jr.

I loved to visit my grandparents in Fort Worth. I'd greet them and put my clothes in my own room next to theirs and race to the cookie jar that sat on the side table nearest the icebox in the kitchen. My grandmother, without a doubt, made the best cookies a boy could ever want. They always had raisins and just melted in your mouth. I could have only one a day without asking so I always took my free pass at the jar upon arrival. I rarely saw my grandmother filling the jar, but it was always full.

In the summer of 1933, however, my parents left me with my grandparents to live while my father worked in Chicago and my mother in Dallas. I learned later that the Great Depression brought about a lot of scrambling for money by many families and often made it necessary for them to travel far in search of work. Even kids had to discover ways of finding spend money with allowances a rare occurrence.

I had three sources of income. I wandered the neighborhood, especially the alleys, looking for wire clothes hangers. I sold them back to a dry cleaner for a penny apiece. I also collected old newspapers, stacked them in the garage, and when I had a big load, my grandfather helped me load up the back seat and trunk of his car and take them to the paper company where they bought them by the pound.

I made most of my money by peddling all over Fort Worth such publications as the *Ladies Home Journal, Country Gentleman*, and *American Magazine*. On the side, I bootlegged copies of Bernard McFadden's *Liberty Magazine*, a practice forbidden by the distributor. If I had been caught, I would have lost my job. There was stiff competition from an older boy in the same area selling *Colliers, Women's Home Companion, Progressive Farmer*, and other titles. His main advantage was that he had a bicycle.

If I had a good week I made anywhere from 58 to 62 cents. You had to sell a lot of magazines to make that kind of money. With what I earned I could see a double feature at the Tivoli Theatre on Saturdays, perhaps buy a *Big Little Book* at the five and ten-cent store, and sometimes get a hamburger heaped with grilled onions from a street stand on Magnolia Avenue. Hopefully, I could end the day with one of my grandmother's cookies!

I could almost always get a cookie if I remembered to save some coins for the Sunday collection at the Presbyterian Church downtown where my grandfather was an Elder. With my grandmother watching, I carefully wrapped the coins in the end of a clean handkerchief and knotted it on Saturday when I got home. I knew to have that knotted handkerchief with me the next morning.

Sunday's ritual never varied. After getting dressed and passing inspection, I helped my grandmother lace her corset. Sometimes I had to take off my shoes, brace myself against her back and pulled hard on the strings while she took a deep breath. With this chore accomplished, I joined my grandfather, a former four-term Tarrant County Sheriff, in the garage where we'd polish our shoes from a large bottle of black polish. Meanwhile, my grandmother filled a basket with cookies, cakes, and sometimes fudge or divinity.

Off to church we would go—Sunday school *and* church. During the church service, I sat between my grandfather and my grandmother who held my right hand in hers. Suffering through church was easy because I just concentrated on Sunday lunch at a boarding house near the courthouse where my grandfather had worked for many years both as a sheriff and as a deputy. We served our food family style in bowls full of vegetables and platters of meat and a side table with desserts. People drank coffee or tea or, like me, milk, and on lucky days they would have chocolate milk.

After Sunday dinner, we always drove to an old soldiers' home outside of town where my grandparents visited with the veterans and distributed the goodies my grandmother brought. The smell of disinfectant always filled the air and I remember it still.

There were soldiers from the World War my father had fought in, from the Spanish American War and veterans of the Indian Wars. I met many veterans of the War Between the States, some missing arms or legs, both Union and Confederate. My grandparents seldom mentioned the war. My great grandfather Clark had fought for the South, while my grandmother's uncles, the Putmans, had fought for the North.

We'd arrive back home in the late afternoon. If I had been a good boy, I was often rewarded with an end of the day visit to the cookie jar—for one cookie and a glass of milk. I remember those days vividly and I remember the sights and sounds and the smells of the lifted cookie jar lid. Funny how things like that stay with you.

# Now and Then

## Esther Hughes Burns

On my 88$^{th}$ birthday, my friend, Jesse Burnett, took me to lunch. Getting lost is not unusual any more and with rain plus multiple roadwork detours, you can either get frustrated or relax and enjoy. We chose the latter.

Peyton Gin Road? Why this was Fiskville not too long ago. I must have been six or eight. There was a grocery and feed store on the corner run by the Harveys. Then there were Hoover's and Neans' dairies just up the hill. Then later, Ray, my husband of 64 years, had worked with Carl Rundberg (Rundberg Lane). Other names popped into my head: Yager, Braker, Gault—streets now, but all people I'd known years ago.

Then, as we approached North Lamar and 45$^{th}$ (Highway 81 to Dallas) I looked for the Insane Asylum Dairy and started to hold my nose. Ooooh, how it had stunk! But no more—just trees and grass. Ramsey's Nursery at 45$^{th}$ and Avenue B would have catered to Lady Bird Johnson, for you could have purchased shrubs, trees, and bushes to your heart's content. I also got a peep at Mr. Harris' little grocery at 44$^{th}$ and Avenue B where I spent my pennies for candy at age four and walked over there *all by myself*. It is still alive and doing quite well.

One unforgettable evening my sister took me for a walk in the woods beyond this store. My eyes popped in wonder at what I beheld. It was a castle, unoccupied in 1919 and as mysterious as a fairy tale. In 1942 my son, Ken, romped through the still-vacant Elizabeth Ney Castle. It was his "fortress" and a challenge to climb up the staircases and out on the roof. (I learned later that Elizabeth slept up there on hot Texas nights.) Today, her fine marble statues grace this castle and my Ken sculpts also. His work is in bronze.

The insane asylum (Austin State Hospital) had a small lake at 38$^{th}$ and Guadalupe where mother took my four older sisters and me on picnics. My sisters even wrestled with a tipsy rowboat as part of the fun. Conversely, a not-so-fun night happened when the Rutledge Boarding House, just across the street, burned to the ground.

I remember Daddy holding me as I watched in horror. I remember it like yesterday. Imagine my surprise as we drove by today and here was the two-story frame Rutledge house just standing there as if it had magically sprung up from that fire of 84 years ago! I wonder if it's now *Rutledge Bed and Breakfast*.

The trolley tracks are long gone. A single track throughout Hyde Park, going down Guadalupe from 40$^{th}$ to 27$^{th}$ street, it then became a double track to downtown. Lockhart Creamery was somewhere around 38$^{th}$ Street. I chuckled as it came back to me the evening in 1945 when we went there for chocolate malt. I was just home from the hospital from having little John Clinton. Ray and I got in the car and picked up Ken and Eleanor at nearby Shipe Park.

They got in and Eleanor looked around. "Where's John?"

she asked.

Heavenly days! We'd left our new baby at home!

A two-story fire hall stood on down the street at about 32$^{nd}$. It still stands and has a heritage plaque on it. My curiosity got the best of me so I called the Austin Main Library and learned it was built in 1906 and the Austin Ballet now leases it. Another fire station came to mind, so I inquired about it. It was located on 8$^{th}$ Street between Congress and Colorado and was really an oldie. She said it was built before 1907 and closed in 1938. I remembered it had a two-tiered wooden gallery above but did not recall the wooden tower on top. What was it for? She didn't know and neither did I.

Well, you know, time has dealt well with the 24$^{th}$ Street Methodist Church (University Methodist). Its beautiful architecture and stained glass windows still gleam. My older sisters went there, probably "to catch a feller." Built in the 1890s, it still lends its magnificence to the University campus. However, Mother and Daddy took us three youngsters to the 10$^{th}$ Street Methodist Church on Brazos.

Right across the street stood lovely St. Mary's Cathedral. It was built in the late 1800's by Nicholas Clayton of Galveston fame. About 1923, mother took me to the ground breaking of First Methodist Church at 12$^{th}$ and Lavaca. Later I went to Sunday School in the basement part of the building as they ran out of money, but it was completed in 1928.

Approximately ten years ago, I attended a function there and upon hearing my story, the church historian pulled out a picture of the groundbreaking and sure "nuf," there I "wuz," standing right beside the preacher who had the shovel in his hands and was getting ready to dig in.

Charlie's Liquor Store and Brydon Lumber Company used to stand at 19$^{th}$ Street (now Martin Luther King) and

Guadalupe. We went on down to the Bob Bullock IMAX Theatre at Congress Avenue where the Lewis and Clark Expedition was showing. I glanced down the street to the Capitol and the great city of Austin beyond. Could this be the town where I grew up? The Scarborough and Littlefield buildings sitting catty-cornered at 6<sup>th</sup> and Congress were the only skyscrapers we had. They say Major Littlefield added a half story near the top of his edifice to out-do the height of his competitor's across the street.

I am so glad my parents chose Austin for our home back in 1914 when they moved here from Indiana. Daddy was a salesman for an electrical sign company out of Chicago and Texas was his territory. Not only was Austin the Capitol but also it was beautifully situated with a violet crown of hills to the west.

Also, there were many small parks to enjoy. Wooldridge Park at 10<sup>th</sup> and Guadalupe was where they played band concerts and political speakers had their say. We little kids slid down the hill in cardboard boxes. The teenagers walked around the square, making goo-goo eyes at each other and the grown-ups settled down on quilts spread out on the grass. A huge tower light beamed down on the whole scene. One night in May 1930, history was made on this corner.

James Fowler, age 11, and two friends were on their way home from playing in Wooldridge Park. James's friends dared him to climb the tower light declaring him a sissy if he didn't. Well, he did and his foot slipped just as he reached the top. He fell 150 feet to the landing below without breaking a bone.

Years later when serving in World War II he was dubbed *Tex* by his buddies who were used to his tall tales but this one was too much. At James's suggestion they wrote to the city newspaper and had this tale verified. From that time on they believed anything he said.

This park remains empty most of the time but once in awhile a crowd perks it up. In the 90s, a crowd gathered for the 100<sup>th</sup> Anniversary of the Tower Lights. During the presentations, I was mentioned for writing the song *Artificial Moonlight* and three of us were asked to sing a trio.

Well, there were other parks around and they're still here today for us to enjoy. Daddy considered Austin the cultural center of Texas because the University of Texas offers so much to the city.

Whatta life! Now at 88 I anxiously wait to see what the future holds.

# My Acre of Dreams

## Roy A. Henley

I stood near the edge of a deep canyon as the sun slowly disappeared below the horizon. Its leaving proclaimed the end of another busy day and I was bone-tired. My accomplishments had been many, so now I could relax; my day's work was done.

Standing beside me was my dog, Butch, a Heinz 57 Variety mutt that followed me wherever I went. It never mattered to him what we did each day as long as we did it together. Butch was very likely the perfect companion. He didn't eat much, mostly taking care of his own needs. He never complained about the weather or the hardships we faced, but he was always there, ready to defend me to his death if danger threatened.

As I started toward my cabin, the canyon suddenly filled with the sound of yelping coyotes. Their primal calls gave thanks for the promise of a bright moon, and warned the local rodents to beware; they would soon be hunting for their evening meal. Somewhere in the distance, the majestic voice of a great horned owl encouraged members of its species to join the hunt. From the brush, the frightful sound of a

31

rattlesnake cautioned us all to stay away from its personal space.

The fading sun shrank to red fingers of light refracting across the darkening sky. As I paused to marvel at its beauty, a voice from the shadows called my name: "Come inside, Sonny, and wash-up. Supper will be ready soon."

The sound of my mother's voice broke the spell I'd been under that day, returning me from some bygone era to the mid-twentieth century and the true reality of my surroundings.

A child's imagination is a wonderful thing. It allows one to experience days filled with bold adventures. I had just experienced such a day!

# *The One Room Schoolhouse*

## Glenn Dehlin

Like the country churches and isolated old barns that dot the Minnesota prairies, the one room schoolhouse, a vestige from the past, is slowly disappearing from the country skyline. They stand alone in seas of tall grass and weeds in need of care that seldom arrives. In the early 1900s, the school was a center of activity with classes five days a week, along with school and farm meetings in the evening. Schools were some three miles apart so children would not have too far to travel.

As with many country schools, the District 11 schoolhouse that I attended was a small, square, white building with a front gable to give it an architectural flair. Concrete steps led to a foyer that opened to the left for the girls' cloakroom and the right for the boys'. The main schoolroom had single desks secured together and lined up one behind the other. The desks had inkwells and places for pencils and the top opened for the storage of books and papers. The teacher had a desk in front of the room. Blackboards lined the walls and the smell of chalk and erasers permeated the air.

As with most one-room schools, the pictures of two of our great presidents, Washington and Lincoln, stood guard over the room. They seemed to wait for the laughter of children to return. It will never happen. On the wall sat a pendulum clock that long ago stopped keeping time. It hangs silent, and why not? No one listens anymore.

The American flag hangs on the front wall where it has hung for decades as an enduring symbol of a proud people unwilling to close an important chapter of education in rural America. The Ten Commandments on the front wall provide guidance for the teachers and students. Though dusty and faded, they remind us of the beliefs of those who settled this great country many years ago.

I attended the same one room school for all of my first eight grades along with about 30 other students. I had several teachers during the eight years of country schooling. They were Mary Curran, Jeanette Lokken and Sadie McGuire. The teacher that I remember most vividly was Mary Curran. She was a good teacher and a very kind and caring person. She would be teaching one group of students and then suddenly switch gears and give her attention to other children of a different class level needing help. As books became outdated, she would give them to us to take home and keep. This would help us as we could do a lot of reading at home.

She didn't just teach. She had to arrive early to a cold room and rush to get the heater going using either wood or coal. By the time students arrived, the room would be reasonably warm, though we had no electricity or plumbing. It did have two indoor type septic tank rest rooms. There was a well, but it never worked, so we hauled water from a neighborhood farm. My mother also taught at one of these country schools, and in some of her journals she lists the pay at $30.00 a month.

We carried our lunch from home in half-gallon pails. We each had a mark on a pail to identify the owner. Mother would pack the lunches in the morning, but I am sure she lined up the lunch items in the evening. She wrapped the sandwiches in wax paper that came with grocery items. At one time, we used "certo" bottles to carry liquids like milk, juices or soup. When we got teased about the certo bottles, we quit using them.

We warmed the soup by putting it in a pan of water on top of the stove. We did that in the morning, and by noon it was good and hot and we generally ate our lunch at our desks. School hours were from 9:00 A.M. to 4:00 P.M. with an hour lunch period. We had a 15 minute recess in the morning and also in the afternoon.

Of course, we had report cards and we would have to get one of our parents to sign the card. We took tests from time to time but the most important test was at the end of the year. It was a standardized test given by the State of Minnesota and we eagerly awaited the results. I never had a problem passing, and sailed through the eight years on schedule.

Transportation to and from school sometimes became a problem. Generally, we walked the mile both ways to and from school. Some of the students rode a bicycle to school. We didn't ride a bike because we had one bike for the eight of us, and never brought up the subject. Many days, we encountered ice and water in the ditches. We would test the ice, and occasionally the ice would break and we would be wet from the knees down. Sometimes we would be wearing overshoes, and we would wade into the water to see how far we could go with out getting wet. Many times we got wet.

Winters were severe in Minnesota. Sometimes we used a

sleigh with horses to travel the distance to school. We would bundle up in heavy clothes and use foot heaters to keep warm. The foot heater would consist of rocks or bricks warmed by the stove in the house and wrapped in small blankets. Riding in the sleigh was fun! You could hear the snow and ice crack as the two horses lunged forward onto the snow and ice covered roads. The sun glistened on the snow and trees. The cloud of moist breath from the horses was a sign that it was indeed cold outside.

The late 1920s and the1930s were drought years in the Northern Plains. It would seem that rain would never arrive. The crops were poor or non-existent and the wind blew. It seemed that dust was everywhere. Many times the dust storm was so bad it looked like night outside, looking like an eclipse. If this happened when we were in school, many of the younger students would become very frightened. Dust storms became a real problem when it was time to go home. We would just have to wait until the wind calmed down.

Yes, the District 11 schoolhouse still stands on the Minnesota prairie, where it serves as a reminder, how students learned some seven decades ago.

# *Going Back*

## Linda Reynolds

I stare down at the crossword puzzle. A faint ringing interrupts the quietness.

"Sister! Do you remember that old hotel in Seadrift we visited every summer when we were children?"

I answer yes while thinking: *of course I remember it, I'm four years younger than you, my memory is just as good as yours.*

"At the beauty shop yesterday, I overheard it was restored as a bed and breakfast inn. I want to drive you there next Saturday to celebrate your 70th birthday."

I'm so excited about the trip I find it hard to fall asleep each night. Finally, the morning of the trip arrives. As I carry my small bag to the car, my sister is asking the usual questions: "Did you remember to bring your pills?" "Do you need to go to the potty before we leave?" Joy has always been like a second mother to me.

It amazes me how Joy can drive fast, talk and gesture at the same time. She enjoys talking about her job. At 73, she still works! She says her new boss looks like a teenager. He wants to get a computer for the office.

"I told him it's absolutely unnecessary. I've managed to keep the company's books for thirty years without one."

As we near the Gulf, we roll down the windows and the sea breeze hits my face. I touch my cheek and remember how this breeze always makes my skin feel like salt water taffy. I inhale the air so deep it lubricates my joints. Joy stops the car and we step out and stretch. I look in her direction. Momentarily she transforms into a young woman with long braids of auburn hanging down her back.

"Sister, I can see the Inn and its just as I remember it!"

I see the long porches that stretch across the front of the two lower levels of the white frame hotel. I think of Papa and his buddy rocking on the downstairs porch and exchanging World War I stories. The parents of Papa's buddy are the original owners of the hotel. I recall the invitation for our family to occupy the entire third story of their hotel as non-paying guests each summer. I smile as I remember the laughter as the family piles into the car to leave the hot, humid city of Houston behind. It's the only vacation my parents had.

I gingerly climb back into the car for the short drive to the inn. When we reach our destination, Joy is still talking as she parks in front and helps me out of the car.

"The sign by the entrance says: "Established in 1908."

At the front desk, the new owners greet us with a plate full of freshly baked brownies before showing us to our room on the third floor. Two young girls bound past us as we slowly climb the stairs. Joy reaches the room ahead of me and is oohing and aahing about how pretty everything is.

"It's so fancy, much fancier than the original!"

On close inspection, I see the once painted panels are now covered with paper. When I mention how cool the sea breeze felt when we opened the windows and transoms on the doors, the new owner snickers.

"We're air-conditioned now and the windows and transoms are nailed shut. If we let the sea air in here, all the wallpaper would fall off!"

We are anxious to go outside and breathe in that sea breeze that is such a detriment to wallpaper. As we make our way down the stairs, I have an impulse to slide down the banister. Mama's voice echoing about proper conduct in a public place restrains me.

We hold hands as we cross the road to the beach.

"Remember how Papa used to fix us up with a cane pole and string?"

I look down at my feet and my shoelaces are untied. I slip my feet out of my shoes and go to the water's edge. Naturally, Joy does what I do. Oh, the pure delight of having the cool sand beneath my toes and the ticklish sensation when my feet sink as the sand is washed from under them. We stroll down to the pier barefooted.

A shadow on the porch beckons for the two of us to come to dinner. We sit at a table for two next to the large dining table that they always reserved for our family. Joy directs my attention to a young couple, the only other residents in the inn, sitting at the table across the room.

"They look like they think they're the first in the whole wide world to discover sex."

When we finally stop giggling, Joy reaches over and wipes the ice cream off my chin.

After dinner, we sit in rocking chairs on the second-floor porch and absorb the moonlight. Joy begins a little game of naming songs about the moon. "Moon over Miami," "Blue Moon," "Old Devil Moon," and "Moonlight Sonata."

Our host steps out on the porch.

"I thought I heard my granddaughters out here."

It's time to go into bed and as usual, Joy has the honor of naming the final tune.

"Moon River."

We snuggle in the covers of the bed. I'm not sure if it's the hotel's floorboards or my bones that begin to creak as they settle down for the night. Joy gently taps me on the shoulder.

"I wonder if the inn's haunted?"

I'm about to tell a ghost story when I can tell by Joy's heavy breathing that she is sound asleep.

After breakfast, we decide to take the long, scenic route to Houston. Joy drives slowly. We pass birds standing at attention on stilts in the marshy flatlands. The air loses its salty smell and we roll up the windows and turn on the air-conditioner. Words seem like an intrusion upon our privacy.

"Sister, we're back."

# Grandmother Johnson's Trip Around the World

## Deanna Johnson Lockett

"Start in the middle and piece the squares around until you have a quilt top to fit the bed," Grandmother said in a matter of fact way. This was her explanation for the quilt top she was working on. I later learned the pattern she was using was called *Trip Around the World.*

She used other patterns but I remember this pattern most. Grandmother made these quilts using squares. One quilt had small squares, another larger squares. These multicolored squares intrigued me as I watched her put them together.

Grandmother Johnson never traveled far from home, and certainly not around the world. She taught me how to sew and she made many of my dresses. Following her instructions, I used her foot pedal sewing machine to make a dress when I was eleven years old. She did not use patterns, but took a few measurements and cut out the dress pieces. She'd cut the leftover fabric from all our homemade clothes into pieces for quilts. The finished quilts covered family members on cold winter nights. I enjoyed picking out the squares that were like my dresses. It was fun also to find Granddaddy's shirt fabric

41

and Grandmother's dresses or apron material.

As a preschooler, I remember playing house with my doll under her quilting frame as it hung from the ceiling. Grandmother, mother, an aunt and other ladies sat in chairs around the quilt. Their legs made walls around me. They laughed and talked and quilted her fabric pieces. The quilting bee ladies were having fun above while I played beneath the soft fabric.

Life was simpler in some ways. We didn't rush here and there attempting to accumulate things, take vacations, or keep up with a fast moving world. Most folks were content to stay home. Occasionally Grandmother would travel a few miles from her home in Ringgold, Georgia, to Chattanooga, Tennessee to visit relatives. Someone else would have to take her because she never drove a car.

Grandmother Allie Alabama Patty was born in 1894. She married Mitchell Johnson at seventeen, and lived her life in Ringgold. Frequently she would .visit a sick or "shut-in" person, or a poor family in the community, or a new mother. I occasionally tagged along. She would take a pie, some freshly churned butter, or vegetables from her garden to share with these people.

I can still remember seeing her with gray hair peeking out from under a black gingham sunbonnet and wearing a bib apron over her simple dress. Everyone knew her as Miss Allie. She kept some of her quilt squares in her apron pocket. While visiting her relatives or friends, she would pull the squares from her apron, and piece them together with a tiny needle. She would sit other times listening to her favorite radio program, *The Guiding Light*. I suppose her mind traveled with the characters on their adventures as the Trip Around the World squares traveled through her skilled fingers.

Life was simpler, but Grandmother worked very hard. She and Granddaddy reared five children during the Depression including my dad, Ralph Johnson. She had some sad times including losing her first child to crib death. She worked hard in the fields alongside Granddaddy all summer, then prepared for winter by canning fruits and vegetables, curing meat in the smokehouse, and in later years by putting things in the freezer. In lean times, she took in ironing for other people, or churned butter to sell for a few dollars. She chose the chickens from the henhouse and prepared them for our Sunday dinners. Thank heavens I can go to the grocery store! I can almost smell those melt-in-your-mouth chicken and dumplings.

Grandmother didn't complain about her lot in life. When I'd say, "I wish I had..." or complain about a chore, she would quote a Bible verse: *I have learned to be content whatever the circumstance.* Philippians 4:11.

She wasted nothing. She used the plucked chicken feathers to stuff pillows. It's amazing she had time to make quilts. This "waste not want not" philosophy carried over into the quilts she made. She used dress scraps, but also cotton calicos sewn to hold flour, cornmeal, or animal feed. They were known as feed sacks.

Grandmother was human and, like all of us, had some flaws. She had very little education and felt that girls didn't need much "schooling." She thought it was a waste of Daddy's money to send me to college. The people of her heritage used words like "hit" for "it," "hissen" for "his." She would "tote" a basket, "reckon" it was so, and go over "yonder." She thought children should behave properly in public.

43

One Sunday when I was a young girl, I sat with Grandmother in church. I must have been wiggling or turned the pages of the hymnal too loudly because Grandmother had given me her "look." I still wasn't fulfilling her expectations so she reached down and pinched my leg, and shook her head to say *no!* She was requesting a change in my behavior.

Well, I was a stubborn little girl and I would show her. I pinched her leg right back. This was not a smart idea! She then pinched me with a vengeance and glared harder. I dared not squeal. The pain brought tears to my eyes, and after a while I let go of her leg. She had won the pinching match, and I knew I'd better be good. Later she explained that I should not distract others from listening. From that day, when I sat with her, I was on my best behavior. *Even a child is known by his deeds, whether they be good or evil.* Psalms 20:11. She was good at quoting the Bible to get her point across.

After Grandmother's death, March 1973, Mother gave me one of the Trip Around the World quilt tops. Mother, Dolores Coombs Johnson, had added a row of sashing to make the top larger. The top was just an ordinary old-fashioned scrap quilt. I had no training in quilting at the time. I decided to tie the quilt.

Since there was no color scheme, I used a variety of colored embroidery threads for the tying. I chose solid lavender color cotton for the backing. I worked on the quilt during a family vacation. We traveled up the East Coast to Canada, and rode a ferryboat that took us to Newfoundland, Mother's homeland, the place where her mother, my Grandmother Mariah Coombs, was buried. I had never met Grandmother Coombs, but I knew I loved her because of the stories my mother told about her, and because I have experienced a grandmother's love.

Though Grandmother Johnson never traveled far, her quilt did. I carried it to Canada from North Carolina. Then brought it to Texas where I now live. I hope to someday take it to Mexico and perhaps other places as well. Then her quilt could truly become a quilt that took a trip around the world.

# *The Polka Dot Cake*

## Linda M. Bonner

On a sixth birthday there's nothing that will make a little girl feel any bigger and more important than to help design and decorate her own birthday cake. My Grandmother gave me this gift along with the honor of planning my own birthday dinner menu in 1950.

It was a special treat to be with Grandmother and Granddaddy on my birthday. They doted on me and were delighted to have me stay with them for the week. Both in their seventies, they were quite active, youthful at heart and mentally acute. Following a lifetime on the farm, they now lived in town. Sadler, a small, rural community in northeast Texas, afforded advantages of being both in town and in the country.

Grandmother offered to prepare anything I wanted for my birthday dinner. I chose fried chicken.

A birthday chicken dinner at Grandmother's began with my selecting from all the hens in the chicken pen the one I wanted to eat. Grandmother's agility and experience made chasing and catching the chicken look easy. She wrung the chicken's neck and as the headless chicken raced about the hen yard flapping its wings, I learned first hand what it means to "run around like a chicken with your head cut off."

Grandmother then hung the chicken by its feet from the clothesline to drain the blood. While she removed the insides and identified each internal organ and its function, I eagerly looked for the fully developed egg, sans shell, which I often found inside. After dipping the chicken in boiling water, she plucked the feathers, with my assistance, and then seared the pinfeathers over the cooking stove's open gas flame. Then we cut the chicken into pieces, for frying.

My second contribution to dinner was going to the garden to select the vegetables I wanted. The biggest treat in this process was being with Granddaddy. The garden was his domain and I felt honored to dig, pick, pull or cut my harvest while under his supervision. I loved the way he talked to me, sharing portions of his gardening knowledge while we walked between the dirt mounds and dug in the rich black prairie soil with our hands.

A birthday cake from scratch began when I gathered the eggs from the chickens' nests in the coop. I didn't enjoy chasing the hens off the nest or cleaning their mess off the shells, but I thought I was big and wanted to do everything myself.

Grandmother's love and patience allowed me great access in her kitchen. I stood on a step stool with one of her aprons tied around my neck, its ruffled hem hanging to my feet. I cracked eggs and poured milk into a huge ceramic bowl. With a long wooden spoon and both hands clamped together in the middle of its handle, I stirred in the flour and sugar, which had been measured from two bins that pulled out and tilted forward beneath the white metal cabinet where I towered over the counter top. Grandmother held the bowl for me and as my arms quickly became weary, she completed the mixing process. Grandmother seldom needed to consider a recipe, but cooked from memory and experience, guiding me with a pinch of salt and a measure of pure vanilla. I was later convinced that I alone had prepared the two-layered yellow cake.

When I asked, "Can I decorate the cake any way I want to?" I received an emphatic "Yes." Thus, with a white icing base, the decorating of the polka dot cake began. .

I responded to Grandmother's question of what colors I wanted on my polka dot cake by citing every color I could think of. She pulled little bowls from the cabinet overhead and lined them alongside the cake. Then came the cake colorings, little vials of the basic primary colors, ready to be added and mixed to the powdered sugar and milk icing we had already prepared.

No matter what color I requested, Grandmother told me how to mix the different colors to achieve the result I wanted. Drop by drop I created every color of the rainbow. Using teaspoons, I stirred and blended the different bowls of icing, each with its special color. Holding each spoon over the cake, I dropped little dots of colored icing randomly across the top. Periodically Grandmother held the cake plate to tilt the cake so I could drip icing in little dots around the side, sometimes dripping several dots at once.

With the purpose, intensity, and precision of Michelangelo at work, I created colors and arranged dots with my spoons, my masterpiece improving with the addition of each new little spot of brightly contrasting icing. Admiring my creation, I thought this was surely the most beautiful cake in the world. My parents' later arrival and compliments of the cake confirmed that this was the prettiest cake ever made and that I was indeed a clever and talented little girl for thinking of and producing something so special.

My paternal grandparents provided a significant influence in my life, modeling respect and trust. My relationship and connection with them contributed to my self-confidence, as well as esteem of others and myself. Their example of enjoying life helped shape my ability to have fun while I worked.

Today I model my own grandparenting skills after those of my daddy's parents. This year, for the first time, I will have the opportunity of helping the two oldest of my five grandchildren bake and decorate their own polka dot birthday cakes.

# Life Begins (A Special Harvest)

## Carolyn J. Scheider

On July 21, 1939, Northwest Iowa residents anticipated another hot, muggy summer day. Like July days of any year, the farmers planned on another typical day of threshing—the one big highlight of the season.

The threshers, working in groups of ten, bonded as they worked. Miles between their individual farms isolated them, so threshing season gave them an opportunity to develop a special camaraderie. It gave them a chance to work as well as play together.

More than anything, they looked forward to the noon meal where they could visit and enjoy a hearty meal together. The wives bent over backwards to cook the best meal of the year for their hardworking, hungry, "meat and potatoes" men.

Their dinner table conversations generally revolved around the harvest along with laughing and carrying on about the latest gossip or joke. But not on July 21. On that day they had me, a special kind of harvest, to talk about. Just one hour earlier, Mom, one of the ladies who usually cooked for them, had birthed me.

With the family doctor's and his nurse's help, Mom

delivered me at home. The farmhouse had no indoor plumbing, making the doctor's and nurse's job more challenging. While electricity had just been turned on two weeks before, Mom had no electric fan much less air-conditioning to lessen the intense heat. This added to the discomfort of the birthing process. In spite of it, Mom and I did well.

As the threshers prepared to go back to work, they closed their meal with the traditional prayer, and thanked God for me. They went back to work with cheerful hearts, recognizing the uniqueness of the day.

For Mom, Dad, and my two big sisters, that ordinary, stifling hot day turned into an extraordinary, bright, miraculous day.

Together they decided on a name that announced to the world how they felt about me. They chose a name that reminded them of cooler weather, and of the joyous Christmas season. For them, this day seemed like Christmas in July. They thought of me as a priceless gift —a gift that made them want to sing with joy. Thus my name, Carolyn Joy.

I've always loved my name, and I appreciate it more and more as years go by. Tough times come and go but I know I bear a name that reflects joy and I have a responsibility to live up to what my name represents.

# The Games Children Played

## Joan Tessier Hollier

The games children play speak eloquently of the times in which they live. Growing up in the 30s in rural Louisiana, we played team sports at school, but at home we played peek-a-boo with the babies, hide and seek indoors and out, blind man's bluff, tag, red rover, king-king-calico, marbles, dodge ball, hit the can. These games required nothing more than active imaginations and space for playing.

Many of our games had the function of keeping older children engaged in entertaining younger ones. On long summer evenings, my sister and I entertained a younger child by holding each other's wrists to form a seat for carrying a smaller child. In the late evening we played "going to froggy land," a game in which an older child wrapped an arm around the shoulders of a younger child and placed the hand over the eyes. Holding the child captive, the two turned round and round. After walking with the submissive child along paths around the house, over the yard and pasture, we finally asked the child to guess the location.

In spring, we picked clover blooms, tying them together to make necklaces, bracelets, and tiaras. Later in summer, we watched for four o'clocks to open so we could pick the bright yellow and pink blossoms, stringing them on grass stems to make adornments. While walking one day recently, I detected the unmistakable perfume of four o'clocks wafting toward me and catapulting me back in time. I picked a long piece of grass and some flowers and sitting on the curb made the adornments of my childhood for a little girl.

Our family games posed risk as some of us grew larger and stronger, so boys tended toward pitch and catch with a ball and bat. Girls scratched out hopscotch squares on bare ground, each treasuring a carefully selected piece of broken glass for a marker. These brightly colored pieces of glass went to school to continue hopscotch there.

Each little girl also had her stash of jacks and a ball that went with her everywhere, safely stored in a Bull Durham tobacco sack with the handy drawstring. At home, we played jacks on the smooth boards of the front porch, although the slight slant of the porch made the ball bounce crookedly. At school, we kept a short piece of a wide board on which we played, hiding it along the fence, returning each day to eat our bag lunches and play jacks during the noon recess.

In addition, we each owned a personal length of rope for jumping. We jumped alone, or two turned the rope for a line of jumpers, or turned double ropes for really skilled jumpers. Adventuresome jumpers got "hot pepper" as we turned the rope as fast as we could. The school children counted in jacks and in hopscotch, "onses, twoses, threeses, etc." My mother always corrected us at home, saying, "Ones, twos, threes, etc." At school I said what the children said, at home what Mama said.

For a preferred activity in summer, climbing trees, we frequented a grove of three gum trees in the front pasture.

Mother sent us out to play when she joined the babies for an afternoon nap. The trees grew far enough from the house to allow children to shout and yell without fear of committing the dreaded sin of rousing her. Only one of the gum trees had limbs low enough for us to get into the tree, but several branches that allowed us to choose different routes into the sky, each of us attempting to go higher than the others. Each year we grew bolder and stronger, and the tree grew higher, challenging us to greater risks. Eventually we found that we could throw a rope over the limb of almost any tree and pull ourselves up into it. None of us ever fell or was hurt climbing trees.

Christmas always opened up avenues for play. Once I received a teddy bear that was ruined by rain when my brother threw it onto the roof of the house. Loss of Teddy bothered me less than the harsh physical discipline my brother received. Although we got few toys as gifts, we played dodge ball until the new ball sprang a leak. We played marbles until all the marbles got lost, and the boys wore out the knees of their overalls. We played with the celluloid dolls until we pressed too hard and caved in the face or tummy. The eyes that closed when composition dolls were put to sleep usually sank into their heads in a few months, and rubber bands facilitating movement of the articulated arms and legs broke. Dresses for paper dolls got torn or lost, or the dolls got left out in the rain. The faux pearl necklaces shed their skins, or the thread broke and dispersed a cascade of beads.

We made our own slingshots and rubber guns, a seesaw with a board and a block of wood, a swing of rope hung from a tree. Flat whiskey flasks or Prince Albert tobacco tins cruised the roadways we marked off under the house. We made a system of levees in the dust of the lot and pumped in water to cause floods and breaks, creating our own system of rivers and bayous.

We loved to play in summer rainstorms, seeking relief from the overpowering heat. We ran with barefoot delight over the pastures and meadows with the driving rain slashing our faces. We stood under the torrent pouring from valleys in the roof of the house. We waded ditches carrying heavy streams of water and splashed in puddles and ponds where water pooled in the cool green grass. When the rain ended, we dried off with rough Turkish towels and snuggled into dry, warm clothes.

In a family of six children, we had no need to seek the companionship of neighborhood children, and other families invariably had a plethora of children and sought no more. I had chums at school, but I seldom visited their homes nor they mine. Our life on Fordoche Bayou was restricted socially to family activities and our lessons, plus brief recesses in school. Because of the difference in education and cultural background between our family and our neighbors, our parents fostered in us a sense of having a destiny not shared by our playmates. Our parents kept us apart from them, allowing limited access under carefully controlled conditions. However, the entire community came together for school programs and inoculations.

The school furnished the community with a social center. The public health nurse came yearly to inoculate us against diphtheria, typhoid, and smallpox. One December before I started school, the public health people arrived to show a movie about tuberculosis and other communicable diseases. They must have brought a generator to power the movie projector, since the community had no electric service.

For me, the wonder of the movie was rivaled by the amazement of seeing the only Christmas tree in our entire community. No evergreen trees grow in Louisiana's swamps except for an occasional cedar used for the school Christmas tree. Farmers kept secret the location of red haw trees and clumps of mistletoe, saving them for the school Christmas. I feasted my eyes on the brilliant riot of color decorating the tree, the shining tinsel, the glowing red berries of the haw, and the smoky foliage of mistletoe.

Occasionally a traveling show got permission to set up in some farmer's pasture to show movies, put on acts with small animals, or play out brief dramas. Sometimes, when our parents' personal curiosity overcame their sense of caution, they allowed us to mix into the crowd that gathered at these events.

I rack my brain for memories of adult social activities in this community. My parents never played cards, got together with another family for a picnic or dinner, nor went to dances. Mother visited with neighbors on rare occasions to exchange cuttings, plants, or seeds for gardens, to share patterns for sewing, to discuss beginning the catechism classes she taught each year. Daddy met the men of the community when he took corn to the mill to be ground into meal and grits, and during Prohibition, he knew where to find the local bootlegger. The men also gathered to round up cattle. All the animals spent the winter together in the swamp, sheltered from the north winds by the trees. When spring came, every man who owned a horse rode into the swamp to retrieve the cattle, driving them to be dipped for ticks, and separating them by brands to return to their home farms.

Actually, work on a farm occupied the time and energy of country people to the extent that little incentive for entertainment remained when the day's work was done. Children's chores and school likewise took time and exhausted our energy. Small wonder that children of my generation became task-oriented adults holding nonproductive activities in disdain.

# *Playing with Trains*

## Anne Zesiger

In small towns during the 50s, families entertained themselves. We didn't go out to eat or to the movies very often. Instead, Mom and Dad created a wonderful play area at home. They encouraged our creativity with the things we had at hand. Dad had a fascination with trains, which he encouraged in his children.

Friday nights at our house in Pampa, Texas were exciting. Pat, Joe, and I would wait for Dad to come home so that we could start assembling the American Flyer train sets. We'd remove everything from the dining room and position plywood boards on blocks for the tracks. Dad would spend the evening scooting around on his back under the platform making sure all wires were connected and attached in the right spots. Many times Mom would also help, with us hanging around the edge of the plywood urging them to finish up. We would anxiously wait for the first train to run. My brother, my sister and I were Dad's "helpers," but were probably in his way much of the time.

Once we completed the preliminary work, we had to decide which train to run first. We could choose the freight train, the passenger train or a combination of trains. Of course, we all wanted our favorite train to go first. As we debated, we set up the village buildings and the railroad-crossing lights. We also glued down shrubbery to make the display as real as possible. We set up each train on the track making sure we placed the wheels in the right spot.

Many times we ran several trains simultaneously. The freight train would start with its tank cars, automobile cars, hopper cars, piggyback cars, log cars, and caboose. Next came the Atchison, Topeka, and the Santa Fe passenger train with its observation car, dining car, baggage car, and Pullman car. Finally, we'd run my favorite, the Ringling Brothers, Barnum and Bailey Circus train which had cars for the wild animals, sleeping cars for the performers, a dining car and baggage cars for all the equipment.

We'd add smoke pellets to the engines, switch the tracks so that the trains wouldn't run into each other, and sit back and watch them run. The sound of moving trains and blowing whistles mesmerized us. We dreamed about the exciting places that trains might go. At night, we'd turn off the lights in the dining room to see all the lights in the engines, passenger cars, and caboose. Each engine had its own whistle that would sound as it approached a crossing.

We loved to control the trains and set the speed of each. Eventually one car would run off the track, and we all helped fix the car. As soon as we placed the car back on the track, the trains would start up again.

For days we had to walk very carefully around the outside edges of the plywood. We were not allowed to walk across the boards for fear of disconnecting the wiring, cracking the plywood or causing a train to derail. Houses and train stations stood along the track.

Dad worked hard to keep our trains running smoothly.

Occasionally, he brought home the latest train or the newest car from Amarillo Hardware to add to our collection. At Christmas he'd surprise us with new additions for our set. There came a time when we returned the trains to their packing boxes and stored them away. All the wires were disconnected and the buildings placed in their boxes, and the plywood was returned to its proper storage place in the garage until the next time. We would then anxiously wait to set the trains up again in the future.

Every Sunday night, Dad would take his hardware orders to the train depot in Pampa and mail them to Amarillo, Texas. We loved to watch the trains with Dad. As each freight train approached the station, it would slow down, but not stop. In the mail car a man would lean out and grab the mail sack hanging from a special pole along the track. This family activity added life to our setting up and playing with trains in our dining room.

# The Gift of Memory

## Ray Bronk

The approach of Christmas always brings me pleasant childhood memories; nostalgic glimpses of events that helped shape and mold me. Let me share one of those interludes with you. Come back with me to a night in the early 1940s, to a narrow snow-packed country road. My older brother and I and six of our schoolmates are walking home from a Christmas Eve pageant attended by us and our classmates. We have just left the warmth of the two-room school several miles south of the tiny village of Custer, Wisconsin.

We are alone, unsupervised, and unafraid, even though the oldest of us is probably no older than twelve, and some are as young as nine. The grown-ups who attended the pageant have left, unworried about us, and have long since departed in automobiles coaxed to life by drivers skilled in frigid-weather magic.

Somewhere, far away, a great war is raging, and sons, fathers, husbands, and uncles are killing and dying. Each day the radio and newspaper bring news of death. We fear for their safety. Tonight however, only thoughts of peace and happiness, home, family, and love linger in our innocent, young minds.

The night is bitter cold and still, with no howling wind to disturb the quiet that surrounds us. The lights from millions of stars pierce the black velvet sky. A giant full moon has risen, and it lights the frozen fields around us.

We imagine that Bethlehem's fields could have looked as peaceful as these. When we pass through places where huge snowdrifts have grown, we walk through 12-foot deep passages carved by snowplows, huge canyons that dwarf our tiny group.

We are a well-dressed crowd—if you consider that we are well bundled by hand-me-down clothes against the cold—and we are in no discomfort. Our warm, five-buckle rubber boots grip the packed snow that covers the roadway. The temperature around us is so far below freezing that the snow creaks and squeaks under our feet as we march in unplanned cadence. This rhythm, the mood, and the exuberance of our group remind us of carols we'd sung earlier. We break into song, harking to herald angels, using the beat of our pounding feet to pace the tune.

The silver smoke of our breath wreathes our angelic heads as our voices soar in the joy of the season. One song leads to another, and soon, the miles have passed and our choir sheds voices as members reach their homes.

Maxie leaves first, dashing up the long snow-packed path to his front door, then the two sisters, Ramona and Betty. Soon, Harold and Dickie depart, and finally, clear-voiced Arlene waves a quick good-bye. This is a signal for my brother and I to race the rest of the one hundred yards to the little white house our Daddy built for us before he died.

We explode with exuberance through our kitchen door, and our warm house and family welcome us. Our chilled noses detect the aroma of the before-bed snack our mother has prepared for us and our younger sister and brother. We hurriedly discard our boots, shrug off our heavy coats and sweaters and hang them on pegs in our bedroom. We plop down on the bench at the kitchen table, and with excited voices, report all the delights and pleasures of the evening.

Moments later, we savor hot, fresh-baked bread with butter and hot cocoa and milk. The pleasant view of our beautiful Christmas tree, the chatter of the family and the delicious food, lulls us into contentment. We are confident that somehow, Santa and for us knowing older children, our mother and aunts and uncles will provide surprises in the morning. We are blissfully unaware of our poverty.

Our sleepy young minds could never conceive of a sanctuary more secure than our little, wood-stove heated kitchen and the loving family and home that surrounds us. Even today, so many years later, those feelings of security and contentment have rarely been eclipsed. It is gratifying to realize that even in these modern times, in millions of young hearts, in millions of different locations, seemingly unimportant holiday experiences are being lived. And, it is a blessing that they, too, will be elevated to "precious" status by a mysterious and benevolent selection process, to be recalled and relived and shared as cherished Christmas memories.

# Christmas Memories

## Ruth Niedermeier

I'll take one more sleigh ride down the hill and then I'll go back to the house to help Papa pile this week's supply of wood next to the house. Pulling my sled and walking back to the house, I wondered about the mysterious lights that danced in the sky. This was the third night that I had seen those strange, silvery, eerie lights. Each night they seemed brighter than the night before. It seemed like the moon was lighting up the whole earth and yet there was no moon. How strange! Sometimes they looked pinker where the sky met the earth, but mostly they were silvery and white. Tonight I would ask Papa about the lights when he reached the house.

"Papa, why are there lights in the sky every night?"

Papa said, "Those are the Northern Lights, the lights from Santa's ovens. He's baking Christmas cookies. He has so many to make for children all over the world; he has to start baking them in November, to get them all baked by Christmas Eve. If children are naughty, he'll turn off his ovens, the lights will disappear and he'll stop baking cookies."

Every night I checked the sky to make sure there were Northern Lights, imagining all the wonderful cookies that Santa was baking for Christmas. I looked forward to Christmas morning when delicious decorated cookies would cover the kitchen table.

# *There is Always Spring*

## Lita De Los Santos

"Wake up, mija, wake up."

I felt the gentle shake as my father's hand urged me awake.

Looking up I could see him holding the kerosene lamp in one hand as he continued to shake me. "Get dressed," he said.

The light shining in my eyes, I put up one hand to shield them from the light. I struggled to wake up. I sat up rubbing the sleep from my eyes and heard Mamma sit up in bed, her voice anxiously asking, "What—what is the matter—what is happening? ¿Qué pasa?"

And Papa's calm voice answering, "Nada, it's all right. Nothing is happening. Nothing is wrong. I'm taking her to the orchard. It's time, go back to sleep."

Still sleepy, I struggled to get into my clothes and wondered why we were going to the orchard. What were we going to do? And why did we have to go now, at this hour? What could we see in the dark?

I looked out the window and saw nothing but the dark, cold morning. The sun was not up yet. And what did Papa mean—it's time—what time? Time for what?

65

Papa handed me my shoes and I pulled them on without socks. Mamma was not looking. I stood up from the warm bed wishing I could crawl back into the warmth of the cozy bed that I shared with my little sister, who now laid snuggled warm under the huge wool quilt. The room was very cold for Papa had just lit the fire in the big, pot-bellied stove and the warmth was yet to come.

I stood shivering as close as I could to the stove, hoping to warm myself but the stove was still and silent. The whole house was still and quiet. I could not remember it ever being so quiet, but then I had never been up this early and today was Sunday and everybody was sleeping a little later as there was no work in the fields. But why did Papa get me up so early today?

I was one of the youngest in this large family and being only six, I didn't have many chores to do except to set the table at meals and gather the eggs. Did Papa need me to gather the eggs now?

Papa brought me my coat and I, yawning, struggled into it. I rubbed my eyes as he led me out of the sleeping house into the crisp cold morning. Soon we were on the small dirt road that led to the orchard. He walked quickly and I hurried to catch up with him.

He stopped, looked back at me and waited until I was in front of him and then quickly scooped me up on his strong, broad shoulders, piggyback. I was really too big to be carried this way. My long skinny legs dangled over his barrel-like chest. His strong calloused hands gripped my ankles as I held on to his neck as he cut across the field of sweet smelling alfalfa.

The sun was now just coming up, the first rays peeking over the small hills that stood guard over the small farm where we lived. The dew was heavy on the grass and looking down from my lofty perch, I could see the dampness on my father's work pants and heavy boots. Holding the coat firmly around me, I felt warm and safe. We walked this way for a long time, so close, yet we spoke not a word.

The clean, cold morning air had done its job on me. Now fully awake, I could hear the birds waking up the whole world with their songs and I could see small animals as they ate their morning meal. Papa stood still for a moment so that I could see them, and at his first movement, they scurried behind a tree or clump of grass, to come back to finish their meal when we were gone.

This was all new to me. I had never been out this early, had never seen this other world—the morning. Every bit of me was now awake, awake to the sounds and sights of this wonderful new world!

Wide-eyed, I took in everything around me. The birds that flew from tree to tree, the squirrels that ran up and down the trees, the rabbits that ate the sweet new grass contently, their whiskers bobbing up and down as they chewed on the grass. The whole world looked like it had just taken a bath and dressed for church looking clean and smelling sweet. I took a deep breath and could almost taste the sweetness of the morning.

"Close your eyes now and don't open them until I tell you," Papa commanded.

Ever obedient, I held one hand over my eyes in case I should accidentally open them without thinking. I could feel that we were climbing and I knew that the orchard was just over the next hill. I held on and kept my eyes covered. We were close to the orchard where Papa had apple, peach, and plum trees. He must be tired of carrying me, I thought as we climbed the last hill, but then he stopped and stood still for a little while and then in a soft hushed voice he said, "Open them now!"

Slowly I took my hand away from my eyes and opened them and gasping involuntarily took in the beauty that lay before me! Blossoms of every shade and hue of pink filled the orchard. Lush green grass covered the ground making the colors stand out so vividly! Stretching for what seemed miles, the colors blended and contrasted with each other covering the little valley.

The sun, now coming over the hill behind us, caught the dewdrops on the blossoms, sending out rays and sparkles like rubies and diamonds. For those few minutes, I saw all the beauty of this world.

We stood this way for a while as I filled my eyes with all the beauty that lay before me, feeling like a queen with all the world's riches at her feet. I held my arms up and wide as if to embrace all the riches that lay before me!

Slowly he lowered me from my perch on his shoulders and I stood speechless. Never before, or ever again, would I experience anything as beautiful as that.

Holding on to his hand, I tore my eyes away to look up to this strange man, my father, whom I was seeing for the first time as a man. He, who was always so busy, never having time to himself, always doing something—working, fixing, patching, repairing—never had I seen him like this. I could never remember seeing him as he looked today. I held tight to his big, calloused hand.

He stood looking into the valley below us, he in his faded overalls, muddy, worn work boots, patched work jacket and slowly, he took off his oil-stained hat and stood tall, proud. With a sweep of his hat to include the whole little valley before us, he said "Look, mija—look at God's work of art! No master painter could ever paint a picture such as this! This must be what the Garden of Eden was like. He gives us the promise of life each spring, no matter how hard a winter we have. We always know there will be a spring—a new beginning, a new start, a new life. He always provides a time to start over again, to leave our mistakes behind and to start anew. How can we deny God's great Grace at this time or at any other time when we know there will always be this—His promise of life! Look about you and at the beauty of all His creation."

He knelt down on one knee, snapped off some wild flowers at our feet, and with a smile held them out to me. I looked up into his beautiful hazel eyes. "But those are weeds. Mama makes me pull them out of her garden!" I said in a tiny voice as I took hold of them.

"Yes, they are weeds, they are wildflowers, but can you deny them their beauty, just because they are weeds? Here in the wild, they give freely of their grace and beauty. Would you pull them out to die simply because your mother does not want them back there in her garden? Everything and everybody has a place here in this world if we will just accept this and allow every one and every thing to be whatever and wherever they need to be, we would be just as happy as God intended."

To a child of six, the wisdom of his words were lost, but years later they would surface and I would understand their true meaning. My eyes could now see beauty and never would I destroy the wild beauty of flowers nor ignore the song of the bird.

Never will a spring come that I don't remember that lovely morning I alone had shared with my father, always hugging this time with him to my heart. I had shared a time alone with my father. He had taken the time to be just with me to share this beautiful morning—me, alone.

My family was a large one where there was little privacy and little time for anything besides work and chores. Yet, he had taken the time.

Believing I alone had shared something very special, I held this as a secret in my heart, always, until the day of his funeral years later when crying, inconsolable, full of regrets and laden with guilt for not spending more time with him, I felt my older sister's arms around me consoling softly saying, "Remember, there is always spring."

# *Traveling Salesmen*

## Ginnie Voelker

Before the advent of electric refrigerators and thermostats, before convenience stores and supermarkets and the proliferation of automobiles to get us to them, and long before technology reduced life's activities to pushing buttons and depending on electronic wizardry, there were people; all kinds of people. They came to the door selling bread or milk, delivering ice or coal. They came on foot, carrying black suitcases containing everything a homemaker might want, from brushes and cleaning products, to shoelaces and groceries. Others brought their wares and services in wagons or trucks, declaring their presence on the street with jangling bells or shouting voices.

An incessant, metallic clang rhythmically announced the slow moving truck that invaded the neighborhoods. Clang, clang, clang, quiet. Repeat. Over and over. Mile after mile. Homemakers peered through windows, and recognizing the shoe repair truck, hustled to the curb waving shoes with worn down heels or flapping soles. The cobbler carried all the tools of his trade with him. He had cutters for the leather and rubber, heavy thread, hammer, nails and shoelaces. We heard that he used "horse glue," which left a lot to the imagination, but if it fixed our favorite shoes, we didn't ask questions.

This self-sufficient immigrant, who spoke only broken English, carried a remarkable grinding wheel for his sideline of sharpening knives and scissors. Boys and girls gathered around to watch him mend shoes, but the real show came when he worked on dull blades, shooting out blue-white sparks from the contact of metal and grindstone. It was Fourth of July all over again.

Each season brought a new selection of businesses-on-wheels to 221$^{st}$ Street. I loved summer, for then the produce vendor added one of my favorites to his stock. His call of "Straaaaawberries! Fresh strawberries!" penetrated every home and if Mom or Grandma had him stop, I could count on having one right from the box.

Of all the vendors that plied their trade on our cobblestoned streets, an organ grinder with a little trained monkey won the popularity prize. When he planted his one-legged hand organ firmly on the sidewalk in front of the stores and began to crank out his familiar honky-tonk music, it was our call to assemble. We kids ran home to beg pennies from our parents, then stampeded to Hempstead Avenue, eager to join the crowd that circled the olive-skinned man.

The music drew us, but the monkey in a red, brass-buttoned jacket, charmed us. He pirouetted inside the circle, then worked the crowd for all it had. The little moocher placed each coin in his pouch, and then crisply tipped his red pillbox hat, an act that tickled us more than the dance. Sometimes in the passing of a penny, we touched the small, wizened hand, marveling at how satiny it felt, and at the perfection of each tiny finger and fingernail. He had lost the calluses of his jungle kin when he learned to dance and doff his hat for a coin.

When no more pennies were forthcoming, the act ended. The rumpled man jerked the leash, signaling the animal to his shoulder and they left, trailed by an entourage of children. The tune of the organ grinder was no less seductive than that of the Pied Piper. We knew our bounds, but we followed as far as we dared beyond them, then turned homeward, wishing the monkey could stay forever.

# *First Kiss*

## Jane Peppard

It was a very warm day in Wollaston, Massachusetts. The yellow and white daffodils and purple irises filled the air with their sweet fragrances. Moisture still sparkled the ground from the early morning dew.

The sun had quickly heated the cool night air.

I had been digging in my yard, pretending that I was planting my spring flowers. Then, I spied my neighbor, four-year old Jimmy Dowling. I asked him, "Jimmy, do you want to come over and play house?"

"Sure," he replied, and came running over.

I brought my dolls out of the house, Jimmy brought his tool kit and we started to play. I was the mommy, he was the daddy, and the dolls were our babies. We were such a happy family.

After a while, I told Jimmy that we had to go down the cellar to clean up the basement. When I got him down the cellar steps I turned around quickly, grabbed him, and kissed him —Wham! Bam! Full on the mouth.

I'll never forget the startled look on his face. His amazement turned to sheer terror and he broke out in a crying wail. His shrieking brought my mother out of the house.

"Gee, Jimmy, now you did it," I exclaimed. Then he turned and ran home crying to his mother.

His mom came over to have it out with my mother. Boy oh boy was I in big trouble. Mom made me stay in my own yard all week. As a result, I missed the big neighborhood event—the tarring of the roof next door. All the other kids got to taste and chew that delicious black tar chewing gum—even better than the gum from the gumball machines, Adams Black Jack Gum.

That kiss changed my life forever. Jimmy never wanted to play with me again. He only played with the boys in the neighborhood. Since I was the only girl, life suddenly became very lonely.

For twelve years, I saw Jimmy going to and from school. He would cross the street to avoid me. I wondered why.

I'll never forget my first kiss. No kiss was ever so sweet and innocent as that first kiss with Jimmy.

I guess Jimmy never forgot it either.

# *Peeping Tom*

## Ellice Smart

My brother wanted to learn Morse code.

"Let's string a wire from my room to yours so we can practice," he suggested.

We now lived in White Plains, New York. When my dad shipped out to Trinidad during WWII, we became ineligible for the apartment complex in Annapolis where we stayed while he took postgraduate work in Meteorology. My grandmother found us an apartment near her, a scarce commodity during the war.

How could we get that wire between the windows? Even with us leaning out as far as we could and using stiff wires, we couldn't reach. We were five stories up, six if you counted the opening for the underground parking garage.

"We can lower a string down from each window and I'll run down and tie them together and you pull them back up," he suggested. "Then I can attach the wire and we can string it from my room to yours."

This seemed a feasible plan to a 10-year-old girl and her 13-year-old brother. We tied weights on the ends of the strings and started lowering them carefully. Even feeding the lines out slowly the weights clanked against each identical window on the way down so we threw caution out and dropped them as fast as we could.

My brother raced down the stairs and out into the entrance to the parking garage and tied the two strings. I pulled the strings up as fast as I could, which was not quite as disastrous since the weights were off center and did not hit windows. Our mission accomplished, he wired us so that we could use keys or lights to send our code. Now, even under the covers with flashlights after we went to bed, we could practice the code.

One evening we decided to practice using a searchlight out of his window. We could bounce the light off the apartment building across the street.

"Did you see that light?" he asked me excitedly. "Someone is signaling us back!"

We spent the next few evenings trying to find that person with our searchlight.

The next afternoon Mother called us into the kitchen and asked us to sit down. We knew we must have done something wrong.

"Are you two flashing a light at the apartment building across the street?" she asked.

"Yes, we're trying to find the person who signaled us with a light."

She was smiling so we guessed that we weren't in too much trouble.

"Well, I'm afraid that you'll have to stop. It seems that some people over there are complaining about the peeping Toms who are looking into their windows."

We spent many an evening sitting at the window hoping to see a return signal even without our searchlight. In later years, we decided we must have hit a mirror in our original experiment.

A happy postscript: Both of us eventually learned the code well enough to become Amateur Radio Operators and we still talk to each other on the radio, from Massachusetts to Texas.

# The Snake Bite

Janie Kirkpatrick

The school bus was a small van-type that the district had purchased during the war. It was a little cheaper to run because it took less gas and the school enrollment had become smaller, so there weren't as many kids to pick up. It was a lovely fall day, the windows were open, and I was enjoying the breeze flowing through the bus. It had been a good day and my mood reflected it as we bounced home from our game.

Our girl's softball team had a four-year winning streak. The pitcher for the team had graduated the previous year, and I had replaced her. Today had been our first game of the season, and we had won. I was relishing the winning feeling and flirting with the young Indian boy sitting next to me on the bus. Suddenly, the bus pulled over to the side of the dirt road and stopped.

Someone said something about the driver wanting to see if she'd killed the snake she'd run over that morning. Most of the kids on the bus piled off but I paid little attention. Then, I heard someone say, "Nina, that snake is biting you!"

The kids hurried back on the bus and my sister Nina

79

diverted my attention. She was five years my junior and had been one of the first kids off the bus. She sat down and the driver took off towards our house, a little over a mile away.

It was evident from the markings on her leg that she had been bitten and the kids affirmed that the culprit was a rattlesnake. I looked at her and remembered what our teachers told us to do for snakebites. I suggested that someone should cut her leg and suck the venom out. There were no volunteers. My excuse for not sucking the venom out myself was that my lips were chapped.

I sat a moment longer and then said, "But she'll die!" There were still no volunteers. Then, one of the younger Indian boys took the lace from one of his high-top tennis shoes and tied it around her leg above the snakebite.

As we made our way to our house, I remembered that this particular day was the day my mother went to town to do her shopping and would not be home. I told the bus driver the dilemma and suggested that we'd have to go to a nearby neighbor's house to take us the 17 miles to the nearest hospital. So, we drove past our house and went to the neighbor's.

We went in, told her of the emergency. She didn't seem too pleased with the interruption, but agreed to take us. She had a small baby and she had to gather some necessities for the child. She told Nina and I to wait in the back of her car. The bus driver got back on the bus and went to take the other children home. There were no phones to notify anyone of our problem.

We were driving to town, (12 miles of dirt road, five miles of pavement) when I told Nina that we should loosen the tourniquet for a few minutes. She looked at me with determination and fear in her eyes and said "No!"

At that moment, I realized how terribly frightened she must be. I also knew I had not helped any by stating that "she would die."

We drove up to the emergency entrance to the hospital and took Nina in. We explained our situation and they responded quickly. They took Nina to an emergency room and told me to wait in the waiting area. Our neighbor took her baby and went home. She would tell my mother the news when she got home.

The doctor at the hospital was setting a broken leg, but he stopped and treated my sister. They had anti-venom for snakebites. They had to slit her legs like piecrust where we had tied the tourniquet because her blood coagulated since it could not circulate. There's a possibility that the tourniquet saved her life. She spent the night in the hospital but went home the next day. The bus driver brought her a box of candy.

# Snake Under the Bed!

## Sarah Bryce

My precious grandparents, Papoo and Mamoo, tried to keep me busy and happy. Whenever I stayed at their ranch, I learned to cook with Mamoo, knot, crochet and play solitaire, and she even taught me oil painting when I was much too young to be trusted with such a messy medium.

Papoo took me fishing and hunting and allowed me to help him build and paint things like picnic benches and barbecue pits at various spots around the ranch. We did wood carving with a very sharp pocketknife, and Mamoo railed a bit that Papoo taught me to shoot, long before anyone thought little girls should shoot guns.

Being from the South, she also thought I should have learned more lady-like things. Her concept of ladies harkened back to the more gentle times before the War Between the States. She said for example, a lady's name should appear in the newspaper three times: when she is born, when she marries and when she dies. How would Mamoo define Hillary Clinton? As a lady? She would hardly rate a quick sniff. Being a lady really meant something. Can you imagine the uproar when Papoo next taught me to smoke? Perhaps it was all part of learning, and learning to think.

Mamoo made me a thick, hard pillow to sit on when they allowed me to drive their car when I was only eight. Our neighbor boy, Don, had to sit forward and work the pedals while I worked the gears and steered. I was too short to do both that year. As cars were irreplaceable during World War II, they were particularly generous and probably foolish to allow me to drive through three cattle guards, two gates, and over three water crossings.

Jack the dog was just as old as I, but he grew up faster. He was my buddy, my tracker, and my protector. He allowed no one to spank me when he guarded me and my sisters will guarantee, half a century later, that I'm still spoiled. I remember Jack as a magnificent friend, brighter than most people, and totally loyal.

I was thrilled the night Papoo said I could sleep outside alone. In reflection, I wasn't really very far outside, on the front porch, as the chaise lounge was just beside my grandmother's open window. Jack left his spot by my grandfather and slept alongside of me, so I wasn't alone and never felt afraid or even nervous. Which just shows how wrong I was.

I awoke to pink light before dawn illuminating a tiny mother wren as she fed her noisy babies in the birdhouse I had built. Bees worked the wall of sweet peas at the front gate. I happily lay a while taking in the light and sounds, and dry cool air before getting up. I felt divine. As I stretched and wiggled, Jack suddenly snarled at me. Me? I was his precious, protected little friend, but his black lips curled fiercely back from his long fangs.

"Hush, you silly beast." I snapped, but he growled even lower and more menacingly down in his chest.

Stunned I suddenly thought, "He's crazy. Must have rabies! He'd never growl at me!"

But some primitive communication harkening back to the time before speech came to humans emanated from his intelligent eyes. He even seemed to be frowning. He looked intensely at me, then under me, then under the bed, snarling again. Curious, I rolled over to look under the bed I lay on, and looked directly into the cold, black eyes of a coiled rattler. "Snake!" Instantly I pulled myself back and began to think what to do.

The way kids think! First, My grandparents were still sleeping. Second, no porch-crawling rattler would live. I formed a plan, then stood on the narrow bed, walked to its foot and jumped down quickly, putting the screen door between me and that rattler. I whispered for Jack, who with eyes never leaving the enemy snake, sidled over to me. His crab-like walk and total caution emphasized the danger.

I slipped quietly through the door and went inside to fetch Papoo's target. We called his .22 a target, rather than a rifle. I guess I'll never know why he called it that, but Papoo said it was the "best rifle in Christamitie's great green world." Only much later did I realize all his things, like the water from his windmill, his dog, his fishing hole and his granddaughter had the same description. We were all the best in "Christamitie's great green world."

Continuing to tiptoe, I slipped back outside to dispose of this vermin that had invaded our private space. Jack stayed firmly at my side as I knelt to sight in on the snake's head. I knew a .22 would carry a couple of miles, but I didn't consider it would go through the snake and then travel so far. I never even thought about missing what I was shooting at. The way kids think!

The house and porch rails were both stone. When I fired, many things happened very quickly. I killed the snake, and woke my grandparents. That speeding bullet also began to ricochet round and round the porch, zinging and pinging with an uncanny screech. Jack and I hightailed for the hills as fast as we could skeedaddle.

Family legend has it, that after awakening with a scream, Mamoo found she had wet the bed. Papoo, all modesty forgotten, came barreling out of the house wearing short-John's, his language blistering the paint off the walls, including some question as where the devil was the target. I knew it was serious because I'd never even seen his underwear except on washday, hanging in the wind.

From the safety of the backside of the chicken house, I began to rethink my actions. I had only tried to handle things without bothering my grandparents, and I simply forgot how a loud rifle shot before dawn would alarm everyone.

Mamoo was sniffy and distant all day, but Papoo quickly forgave me because, after all, I had killed the snake. "One shot, right through the head," he proudly proclaimed to any and all. I felt awfully proud of myself too. He always added, "I'm the one who taught her to shoot."

Mamoo got over it. I think Papoo's attitude demonstrated how close he was to the Old West, the frontier, and the free attitude that allowed an eight-year-old girl, for heaven's sake, to drive a car and shoot a rifle.

Papoo never had a fishing license, nor paid income tax, reflecting a time when government was smaller and less invasive. Time passed and I learned to think things through a little better, but no one gave me my own .22 until I was in my forties, and too old to care. Without a doubt, those were precious grandparents, and I was so lucky to have those experiences, that helped form the way this kid thinks.

# *Everybody Grows Up!*

## Judy Crawford

When someone tells me the younger generation is going to the dogs, I always smile indulgently. That doesn't mean I'm unaware of the "Zombie-actions" youngsters sometimes pull. Since I have two teen-age sons, "aware" is actually an understated word.

Maybe my boys are lucky because I'm at once conscious of and sympathetic of their heritage, or because I have overactive retentive powers. Since I lived alternately in town and country, perhaps I have double vision of the unlimited possibilities of childhood experiences.

Anyway, I don't even start a countdown when my kids do something weird. If I'm tempted to blow my stack, my memory jets back across all the zany stunts of three generations. I remember my saintly grandma, who stood only four feet ten inches high, and at 94 still had all her teeth, and I become instantly more lenient.

I'll never forget how it shook me as a child when I found out how grandma lost a toe. No ancient infection or anything like that, pure cussedness, that's what! Her brother chopped it off one day when he was splitting firewood. Not that he was any delinquent either. He just didn't think his sister was so ornery as to put her bare foot on the log again after he had warned her three times that if she didn't stop sticking it in the way and tormenting him, she was going to lose a toe. Well, she didn't stop and she did lose a toe.

Next generation, there was my mother who grew up to be as conservative and prim as a woman could be. Yet grandma said she used to keep her own figure trim by fetching back my mother who would slip off and follow grandpa when he was making the 15-mile trip to town in the wagon. She would trail grandpa at a safe distance. If she overtook him before grandma caught her from behind with a hickory stick, grandpa was too kindhearted to make her go back home in such a breathless, faint condition. So she never stopped trying, thinking that 50 percent success was a pretty good average, and that the trip to town was always worth a try.

Now, after that background, you'd have thought that my parents and my cousin Posy would have been prepared for our chaotic childhood and adolescence, but I guess their memory wasn't so good. I don't see how those four dear souls ever survived the shocks we put them through. They must have felt as if they were going down an escalator one minute and on a rocket to the moon the next.

Alone, I was as shy and introverted as a girl could be. Posy, who is slim and lovely now, was plump and ordinary then. But just put us together and there was a chemical combustion. To put it bluntly, we were dynamite and totally unpredictable. The family cussedness raised its ugly head when we were six; probably because that was the first time we were left alone, and only because of the lure of a one-cent sale at the corner drug store. Our mothers thought surely we were ladylike enough to conduct ourselves properly for an hour, but that was just how long we needed.

It all started very innocently with a romp in the back yard, but a perverted fate felled a tiny chick, quite dead, in our path. Although tenderly sympathetic, we were no less practical! What a shame for good food to go to waste with all the poor, hungry children in the world. Our parents had impressed us well with this gem of wisdom!

Proudly, we plucked, washed, cut up, and fried that chick—mind you—just the way we'd seen our mothers do. Gourmets that we were, we made cream gravy (no lumps, either). We set the table, knife and spoon on the right, thank you, and fork on the left. In triumph, we were about to dine when our mothers returned with bulging packages from the annual one-cent sale. The rouge they had tried as samples was not enough to cover the pallor of their faces when they saw those miniature drumsticks. Their soft, refined voices turned to fish-wifely shrieks when we told them under what conditions we had made chicken for dinner.

"A stiff-necked chick—fried!" my aunt screamed.

Posy, who loved to eat, was plainly disappointed. "I guess we should have made dumplings too," she said as we were marched into the bathroom to soak our hands in the strong, hot solution my mother had mixed. Good thing disinfectant was one of those one-cent deals!

Our animal mishaps continued the time we found two six-foot rattlesnakes in the backyard. By the time our parents arrived on the scene, we were already sporting bracelets strung with the rattlers. We had chopped each snake into six-inch lengths and put a brick on each piece. We had heard that dead snakes would wiggle until sundown, and we were determined they wouldn't zig another zag.

Then there was the issue, still timely today, of when to

begin using make-up. Posy and I were most precocious in this matter. When our mothers forbade the use of lipstick and rouge in the sixth grade, we pleased them by placidly accepting our fate and getting dressed a little less languidly than usual in the mornings. That gave us a few minutes to stop in Mr. Porterfield's turnip patch on the way to school to apply what we thought was the subtlest amount of red crayon, innocently tucked away in our satchels. We thought all the winks and notes we got in class showed how wrong our mothers were and how right we were. Of course, we know now that all it proved was how unsophisticated sixth grade boys really are!

We developed our own diet regimen that same year, quite by accident, at first. We discovered that one or two of Mr. Porterfield's crisp, purple turnips, eaten on the way home from school, made us less ravenous at suppertime. They also removed the crayon from our lips. It was along about then that Posy began to lose her plumpness and I did some trimming too. All we had to do was to tell Mr. P. that he had the nicest turnips on the school route, and he beamed and told us to help ourselves. We'll always remember that man! You'd be surprised at how many pounds we'd shed by the end of turnip season. If we had given a transfusion, it would have been pure turnip juice.

The next summer we realized while dressing one Sunday morning that we looked just a bit too rounded in certain spots to be presentable in the House of the Lord. We believed in doing something about a situation once we knew it existed. We hunted in my mother's closet until we found patent leather belts of just the right width. We strapped them tightly around each other's chests and donned our dresses, quite pleased with the flat results. We must have looked deformed, but no one seemed to notice. At least, we were never scolded, but it wasn't long after that until our mothers added another item to our lingerie wardrobe—and without asking! We learned right then that it pays to be resourceful and patient— then parents think that something is all their idea.

I remember the time I became quite ill at school. Always looking for a good excuse to leave class, Posy eagerly offered to walk me home. Since we were not expected until much later in the day, no one was there. By then my breathing sounded so loud and laborious in the silent house that Posy forgot her joy at the unscheduled holiday and became truly frightened, telling me solemnly to hang on, she wouldn't let me die. With that resolved, she very efficiently put me to bed and painted me solidly from neck to waist with what we called "monkeyblood." Since I was too sick to care and never expected to leave the house alive anyway, I lay docile and consoled myself that at least she cared.

When Mother got home and saw the ghastly sight, she was so relieved to find it was only Mercurochrome that she didn't even scold Posy for the state of my skin and the bedclothes. By the end of a severe bout with pneumonia, I finally lost my pinkish color, but the sheets were a total loss. My illness, however, served some purpose. Posy never again complained about feeling too bad to go to school.

There were numerous and sundry other pranks we pulled. I could write an account as long as *Gone With the Wind*, but I think you have the idea. Anyway, I don't want to completely disgrace the family name.

That's why I say my sons are lucky. Any time I feel compelled to react like an over-anxious parent, I just need a second to recall my childhood, and I can see my offspring in the right perspective. After all, you have to be a caterpillar before you can be a butterfly.

Then when the boys do bring home a good report card, help the elderly lady down the street, or go to Sunday afternoon services without being asked, I just say a prayer of thanks, knowing that I have reaped more than I deserve.

On second thought, perhaps I should say a prayer of gratitude that my children aren't girls!

# If One of Us Had Spoken Up, But We Were Both Too Shy

Mary Katherine Earney

Late in the 1930s, I spent a summer in Beverly Hills, California with my Aunt Kitty. She allowed me to do anything I wanted as long as I didn't bother her. Bill Morton, a friend from the University of Texas, called me one morning and asked me out to a concert at the Hollywood Bowl featuring Lionel Hampton and Alec Templeton, the blind pianist. I really liked Bill Morton and my heart soared.

Bill came by that night in a rattly Ford coupe and off we went as the moon shone brightly through the cool night air. Templeton and Hampton delighted the crowd by taking the lead away from each other and playing away. Afterward, we went to one of those new fangled drive-in restaurants, got a coke and went for a ride along the beach. The waves, moon, and Bill hypnotized me.

We held hands as we walked near the water's edge. Shyness prevented both us from saying what we really felt. I didn't want this relaxed happy evening to ever end. Finally, he took me home and we stood at the door talking for a long time. Eventually, I gave up on a good night kiss and said my good-byes. He said he'd call again but he never did. I grew more depressed because I didn't know his telephone number.

I moved on with my life and a few years later married and began my family. Nearly five years later, I went into the post office in Marfa, Texas and the postmaster asked me, "Did that man find you yesterday?"

"What man?" I responded

"Somebody named Bill. Said he knew you before the war."

A few days later a post card arrived that said, "I got through four years of a POW camp by remembering you and what fun we had that evening in Beverly Hills. Love, Bill Morton."

# World War II Homeland Security

## Joy H. Goodale

In years to come, everyone will always remember what they were doing the morning of September 11, 2001. As now, those of us who were here December 7, 1941, remember the moment we heard of the attack on Pearl Harbor.

Our family had gone for their usual Sunday drive after Mom's Sunday dinner of fried chicken, mashed potatoes, green beans, and apple pie. We rode with the windows down in Dad's 1939 Black Ford Sedan. Although it was December, and the first day of winter was just two weeks away, we were enjoying a balmy spring-like day. We usually drove downtown and looked in the store windows. Each of us mentally pictured a Christmas list from all that was displayed. On the way home we had fun exchanging hints about what each of us wanted.

When we arrived home, my brother and sister and I sprawled on the floor to read our library books or finish our school homework due the next day. Mom and Dad sat in their twin rockers talking. Dad lit a cigarette and leaned over to turn on the radio. This peaceful scene was shattered by what we heard on the radio.

"We interrupt this program to bring you the news that the Japanese have attacked Pearl Harbor by air."

Of course, we did not see the immediate images of the devastation, which television provides now, but it was no less shocking. My brother, who was seventeen, was ready to join the service that day. He grabbed a broom, threw it on his shoulder like a rifle, and marched around the living room.

The following week in school we heard over the intercom President Roosevelt's Declaration of War before Congress. His words, "This is a day that will live in infamy," were quoted everywhere. All of the kids were worried about what was going to happen, and wanted to know how they could assist the war effort.

Shortly thereafter, my brother joined the U.S. Army Air Corps. We never questioned our duty to serve our country. Our Dad had served in World War I and, to his death, could recite the number on his army issued rifle. He taught us patriotism and love of country. Now, my brother would be on his way to serve in Europe.

We were all proud of our brother. Looking back, I can see how his departure saddened Mom and Dad. As a girl in my early teens, it seemed very glamorous. Our little sister tried to put a bright face on his leaving by telling Mom it would be easier to cut the pie in four pieces instead of five. She couldn't understand why Mom started crying harder.

We were soon involved in recycling paper and scrap metal and purchasing war stamps. Practically everyone planted a "Victory Garden." Air raid drills were common. At this uncertain time, we did not know if the enemy would invade. Japan or Germany could have done so had they truly known our vulnerability. Families accumulated emergency supplies similar to those we collect today in case of hurricanes such as candles, water, and canned goods. I appreciated this effort but the real answer I was waiting for came the following year.

A recruiter from Ellington Air Force Base in Houston came to our school to tell us about the CAP (Civil Air Patrol). This organization had formed in December 1941 as an auxiliary to the U.S. Army Air Corps. The sudden attack on Pearl Harbor had created an atmosphere of uncertainty. As far as anyone knew, we could be facing imminent invasion of our shores.

The CAP recruited civilians to identify enemy aircraft and thereby guard our borders. Another group formed to fly our coastlines, do all types of offshore reconnaissance, and spot submarines. This group consisted of older civilians that could already fly or could take training to do so. Our high school group learned to spot aircraft and relay information back to headquarters. This appealed to me. Perhaps it made it seem closer to what my brother might be experiencing in the Air Corps.

We were issued uniforms: khaki cap, skirt, shirt, tie and regulation brown oxfords. There were red epaulets on the shoulders. Once a week we had training at Ellington Air Force Base. It was not a game. We were taught Army discipline, how to obey orders and how to march in formation. We were given a manual that depicted in silhouette, the Japanese and German aircraft from fighters to bombers.

After learning this required material, we were assigned the Gulf Coast area around Galveston and the large refinery area at Texas City. Although we were not going to fly, the Ellington Field airmen gave us a ride in a yellow Piper Cub. There's no thrill like flying in such a light aircraft.

When I was home, I ran outside and looked skyward every time I heard a plane fly over to be sure it was a friendly aircraft.

The CAP used Piper Cubs to fly the offshore reconnaissance. This aircraft was usually fabric with very basic instrumentation whereas the planes used today are usually fully metal-covered with better communications and radar.

Robert Neprud has written a book entitled *Flying Minutemen* that details the wartime history of this organization. He has recorded the 18-month record of the volunteer civilian Coastal Patrol.

Neprud states, "During this period it was known to have reported 173 U-boat sightings, sunk two, summoned help for 91 ships in distress and for 363 survivors of submarine attacks. It sighted and reported 17 floating mines and, at the request of the Navy, flew 5,684 special convoy missions."

This was not without cost, as twenty-six CAP aircrew members gave their lives and ninety aircraft were lost.

I continued in this program until the spring of 1945, at which time I held the rank of cadet 1$^{st}$ Lieutenant, a big year: the Germans surrendered in May; the Japanese surrendered in August; and I graduated from high school. I'm proud of manning the country's first line of defense. Although we never spotted any enemy aircraft, we lived the CAP motto: "Semper Vigilans," *Always Vigilant.*

# *My Very First Bicycle*

## Mary Reece Hobbs

My bike is red. I wanted it blue, but I'll keep this one. I'm lucky to get it, Mother said. There's a war going on and no spare rubber or metal for building foolish things. I waited four months for it. I licked a lot of stamps. All the kids buy war bond stamps at school. That's how I got my bike. Licking stamps and pasting them in my war bond book.

My brother, who's in high school, used all my shoe ration stamps. Mother said his feet were growing faster than mine. She cut leather half moons out of my shoes, so I could wear them longer. They don't look so good now. It's fun pasting stamps with the other kids, kind of like collecting baseball cards or marbles.

Some things are not so fun. When the wailing sirens go off, we have to run for the halls and cover our heads with our arms. It scares me a lot. Mother said it's just practice, but my friend Donna said some army guys spotted Japanese bomber planes by Long Beach. Sometimes we go there for picnics by the ocean. It only takes a little while in the car.

Roaring waves slam the sand. I wiggle my toes in the salty water. I look way out for enemy ships. Once I saw a whale. Daddy welds on ships. Not for the enemy but for our army. My other brother is somewhere fighting in jungle islands. Daddy said, maybe, this war work would bring him home safe and sound.

Mother listens to news on our radio in the evenings. She turns knobs this way and that until the static is gone. Then she cries a lot. Wish we could hear only big band music. I sit in my swing outside her window, and pump real hard. Wind whistles in my ears. Maybe if I can swing high enough, I'll reach a magic land where everyone is happy and there's no war.

# Georgie

## Ruth Lehman

It was a Saturday, the day of the week that rural families often packed up the kids in the afternoon and drove into town. Parking along the main street, they strolled along looking into store windows and eyeing people they met on the sidewalk. The ritual reminds me of the paseo found in Spanish cultures. In 1943, before television, it was a welcome diversion.

Two young country girls living on the side of a hill across the railroad tracks from town always looked forward to this event. Sometimes spare change in the family pocketbook enabled the purchase of double-dip lemon ice cream cones at the end of the evening. The family lived in a very simple two-bedroom house without plumbing, central heating, gas or electricity. Water came from a cistern. There was no radio, no telephone, no washing machine, no refrigerator, no vacuum cleaner, none of the town conveniences. However, it was a world without crowded roads and crowded cities; a world where the air was clean, the nights starry, and fields filled with wildflowers.

Two years had passed since the Japanese had attacked Pearl Harbor, but the girls couldn't grasp the menacing mystery of the war. They felt safe, but not beyond the reach of distant battles, because uncles, cousins and neighbors in uniform came home on furlough to say "good-bye" before going overseas.

They patriotically participated in the "war effort" with its scrap-metal and paper drives. Rationing of gas and meat became a fact of life for everyone, but poor farm families like theirs were used to austerity. Rationing of meat, eggs, butter and sugar affected them little since they had always produced much of what they ate.

They took advantage of the opportunity to supply alternatives for rationed food items by raising 25 rabbits and 100 chickens for sale to the A&P store in town. They worked hard and emptied smelly, sloppy trays of rabbit urine, and kept food and water containers cleaned and filled. They plucked and scraped chicken feathers and washed and packaged slaughtered rabbits. Knowing that these creatures ended up dressed for sale at the meat counter, kept the children from making pets of any of them. This family had no place for pets.

One Saturday a few weeks before Easter, Ben Franklin's 5-and-10-cent store offered live chicks and rabbits for sale in impossible colors of pink, blue, and lavender. Strangely, there was one naturally black one among the rainbow colors. The two young sisters, nine and ten, looked longingly at these exotic creatures, wishing it were possible to pick out one each for their very own. The sweet high peeps and hopeful surging of the chicks toward the girls as they approached appealed powerfully to their tender instincts, and they begged their mother to give them a dime apiece for a baby chick.

Perhaps because it was Easter, perhaps because the girls had been helpful and had demonstrated sufficient responsibility, perhaps mostly because caring for two more chicks represented no additional outlay, their mother gave her permission and each child carefully made her selection. Eleanor finally chose a fluffy pink one, and named "her" Nellie. Ruth, the older sister, chose the oddball black one and named him Georgie.

To keep the chicks warm, they kept the chicks in a box behind the coal-burning stove in the kitchen, next to the children's own unheated bedroom. At night, from the bed they shared, the children could hear through the open door, the contented peeping of the chicks as they snuggled together, very much like the children themselves.

After school and after chores, the children took Georgie and Nellie out of their boxes and allowed them to explore the kitchen. The linoleum covered floor made "accidents" simple to deal with. Later, as it grew warmer, the chicks ran about in the yard with the children to enjoy the sunshine and the fresh grass.

Georgie thrived and showed some pepper-and-salt markings as the black down began to turn to feathers. Nellie's pink fluffy feathers faded and began to turn white. But poor little Nellie never grew properly and was never very healthy. We learned later that the dye process itself was the cause. Eventually she died, and Georgie became the petted darling of both girls.

They carried him everywhere. They made booties for his feet and a bonnet for his head. They made a snazzy vest to complete the costume. Georgie didn't mind the bonnet and vest but he found the booties very difficult to walk in. He managed by alternately lifting each of his feet very high off the ground. The girls called it marching. Because it seemed so comical, it was a favorite pastime of theirs.

Georgie grew up to be a magnificent barred-rock rooster. He sported a jaunty red comb and wattles. He had a strong yellow-orange bill and sturdy yellow-orange legs to match, with short spurs at the back. Each of his feathers was beautifully marked, alternating rows of black and white. His glossy tail feathers arched proudly up from his back and then gradually cascaded downward in a smooth plume so long that it draped over his wings on either side. He carried himself very proudly indeed and when he stretched out his wings, he displayed his regal beauty.

Whenever he fanned out a wing, they began to repeat, "Show me your wing, Georgie." "Show me how beautiful you are, Georgie!" After a while, he responded on cue to either prompt by unfurling one of his wings and sweeping it to the floor. They also taught him to crow on command. He never seemed to tire of responding to their pleas: "Crow, Georgie."

Even the girls' mother became very fond of Georgie. She had to work very hard, growing and canning most of the vegetables the family ate, so she frequently worked in the garden. Georgie loved any activity that took place in the garden, and since he had the freedom of the house and grounds, he often scratched away beside the girls and their mother. His unusual behavior seemed almost human.

Once, when Georgie helped himself to a plump ripe tomato still on a vine in the garden, the mother threw a clod of dirt at him and scolded him. He indignantly half ran and half flew across the road, up the hill, and onto the front-porch rail of a neighbor's house. Obviously sulking, he roosted on their rail all afternoon, watching from above as she worked in the garden, and didn't come home until dusk.

Another time, when Ruth was carrying Georgie along a weedy path, he began to arch his neck to one side at an unusual angle and, opening his beak, he made a hollow hissing noise exactly like a snake. As Ruth looked in that direction, sure enough, a snake lay concealed in the weeds by the path. What more proof could be required? Georgie was a very smart and beautiful rooster. The children were extremely proud of him.

He ruled the roost, so to speak, in the family's chicken yard as well. When he found a particularly tasty delicacy, he made a rapid clucking sound and did a little shuffling dance to call the hens to him. It didn't matter that he was a dominant male doing what a male does in the family's flock. However, it mattered very much to another neighbor, who had 200 white Leghorn hens who were producing eggs for sale. Since these for-sale eggs had to remain unfertilized, it caused hard feelings whenever Georgie decided to fly next door for a visit.

Georgie occupied a very special place in the family for about five years. Although he hadn't seemed sick, they found him frozen stiff one winter morning. When the ground thawed they interred him with the respect and affection due him for the years of delight he provided. They would always remember the joy and happiness of those years.

# The Morning After the Night at the Bar

## Lois Earley

In 1944, I was a sophomore in high school, and WWII raged on. I got up early one morning to get ready for school and had just come downstairs into the dining room when someone knocked on the back door. Mother had left much earlier for her job in a small rubber shop and I was alone in the house. The knock frightened me because our little house set back from the street and it backed to the end of a service alley. Fearfully, I wondered who had knocked on our door at this early hour.

I looked through the door curtain and there on the small back porch with morning mist on the ground behind him stood my dad. He had left us when I was only nine and he never came around except at mealtimes, then he came with empty hands and a stomach to match. This morning he waited for me to unlock the door and shifted the hindquarter of a cow he carried on his shoulder. I could hardly believe my eyes.

I let him in and he told me about a friendship he made with a man at a bar the night before. After a few drinks (who can say how many?) the two became old, fast, arms-around-the-neck buddies. They must have talked about all of the shortages brought about by the war and then the subject of rationing came up. We never had enough meat and we had ration books with stamps for any meat we bought. In these circumstances, what do friends do for each other? Well, they help them get what they need. So, they went to his new old buddy's home and shot one of his cows. They spent the rest of the night dressing it and here he stood with an entire back leg on his shoulder.

When Mom returned from work about four o'clock that afternoon and saw what he had left, she was furious. She had been up since five that morning and had looked forward to relaxing a bit before dinner. Now this. We had no large refrigerators or freezer. We had no way to freeze anything except two small trays of ice, and if they froze, the eggs on the bottom shelf also froze. We lived well over a mile from the closest store where we could buy canning jars, and since we had no car, we had to walk to the store and carry the heavy jars home.

The next two nights we put in long hours cutting the meat from the bone and canning it in pink jars. Mom grew very tired from too-long hours and not enough sleep. The kitchen filled with the sickening sight of bloody bones and colanders of trimmed fat and gristle. The first night the summer heat forced us to pack as much as we could into the refrigerator. By the end of the second night, we had many pint jars of diced beef lined up neatly on a shelf in the basement. Eventually, Mom's anger cooled and we had the most tender meat we had had in years, a welcome supplement to our meager meat rations. To my knowledge, this was the only time since he left us that my dad ever brought us anything.

# *In War*

## Herbert Teat

As the sole clerk, I stood sorting mail in the college bookstore/post office. With morning classes in progress the manager took the opportunity to go to the bank. After one year at Hardin-Simmons University on a work scholarship, the boss trusted me to mind the store.

An exception appeared during the sorting of the morning mail. Normally cards from draft boards routinely went unnoticed. By the spring of 1943, the second year of the war, boys all over the country regularly received draft notices. The first notice contained a card with a classification from the Selective Service System that determined where a fellow stood in the draft process to enter into the armed forces.

In the midst of the pile of mail appeared a notice from my Draft Board in El Paso County five hundred miles away. I stared agape at the card in disbelief at my classification of One-A.

The pride of a young American mounted to its highest at such a notice. It confirmed fitness to serve his country. In the process of the draft, this notice preceded the call for a physical examination of each draftee. The fear of the consequences of war never crossed our minds at this time. My pride didn't last long and gave way to the stark reality I faced. I knew my One-A classification would never survive "the physical."

This reality came out of the fact that seven years earlier I began coping with the effects of infantile paralysis, later called polio. The partial paralysis of muscles on the left side of my back assured that no way could I qualify for military duty. I could foresee clearly that a Four-F Classification awaited me, and a loss of my pride.

Wanting to keep a stiff upper lip, I immediately crossed over to the soda fountain and showed my One-A card to Jean Humphrey. Her congratulations showed an awareness of the situation. Jean was engaged to Bill Mauldin, a soldier in the 36th Division of the US Army in training at nearby Camp Barkley. After store hours, with very slow steps, I made my way to Ferguson Hall, the men's dormitory.

Brotherly love between college guys, long remembered, develops in dorms during dominos or card games and "bull sessions." Among males, this closeness often manifests in an expression opposite to inner feelings, yet understood.

I entered the outer room of my dorm quarters during a game of New York hearts. Most of the players had already signed up in the reserves for some branch of service awaiting their call: Milton "Pluto" Hughes, Army Air Corp; Rex Perry, Navy; Mario Palafox, Medical Corp. Bill Healy fell victim to a red tape snafu when in the process of signing with the Navy. The Army grabbed him and sent him overseas before his Navy papers cleared.

I interrupted the game with, "Awright, guys, feast your eyes on this." I proudly plopped my draft card down in the middle of the table.

Healy picked it up, read it, and yelled, "My God, we're losing the war!"

After each read the classification, they stood as one and hoisted me in the air.

Cheering all the way, they carried me, horizontally, down the hall into the dorm floor's community bathroom. While boisterously singing "For he's a jolly good fellow," they suspended me vertically, head first, into a commode and flushed it—twice.

The memory of their expression of goodwill carried me through the aftermath of the physical exam and while I worked in an aircraft factory for the duration of the war.

Every one of them survived the war. I received letters from Infantryman Healy who walked across Europe collecting Purple Hearts and the Silver Star. During the invasion at Leyte Gulf in the Philippines, soon after cleaning up a ship hit by a Kamikaze plane, Rex wrote from his landing ship, "I'm going to spend the rest of my life trying to forget what any fool knows is impossible."

I thank God for the gift of the human spirit that makes it possible to cross the void of time and distance. Nothing can separate us from the close friendships in our memories.

# WWII Newspaper Correspondent

## Nadeane Walker Anderson

When America entered World War II, I had recently graduated from college and now wrote for the *Fort Worth Star Telegram.*

The three youngest of my five brothers had volunteered early–for the Army, the Navy and the Coast Guard. That left the Army Air Corps for me! Because so many newspapermen had volunteered or been drafted, I got great assignments and front-page by-lines on my first job. Though I loved it, I really wanted to join my brothers in service and go abroad.

Specifically, I wanted to go to Paris and write for *Stars & Stripes*, the Army newspaper. That my chances of doing this were worse than remote did not occur to me. I was young and optimistic. Pushed partly by the fall of France and thinking I might not ever have a better chance, I enlisted. I had always had a romantic vision of Paris, and I feared the Germans might destroy it before I got there.

Dreams can come true. About a year later, I was in Paris writing for *Stars & Stripes*. I could hardly believe it!

I had enlisted knowing that my parents would not approve at all, and that many people looked askance at girls in military service. I didn't want to hurt my parents, but I followed my heart.

Everything happened fast. I was assigned to the Air Transport Command and sent to basic training, which I hated. It began with the humiliation of having my long hair, worn tucked into a chic Lily Dache snood, let down and searched for lice, and continued with being shod in stiff, ugly boots that blistered my heels.

I put up with such indignities in the hope of what was to come, and eventually went back in Texas on my first assignment to Love Field in Dallas. One of my best friends in college had also enlisted and arrived at Love Field not long after I did. I learned that Vernelle was there when I heard the girls laughing about a new recruit who had dropped her cap in the soup in chow line

After a few months, we started to ship out, most to US posts, but some abroad. I squeezed onto the final list for Europe, certainly helped by determination, luck and perhaps a fairy godmother.

At Christmas, I froze in a cold barracks in New Jersey, where one of my friends got in trouble for insisting on wearing an Army blanket over her uniform. Next, we found ourselves in the bowels of a troopship, bucketing through foul weather and the threat of enemy U-boats towards a landing in Wales. Seasick all the way, sliding from one end of the mess hall to the other in our lurch and tilt progress, we slept in our uniforms with our boots on. One night we turned out on deck ready to climb down rope ladders into lifeboats, until the blip on the radar turned out not to be a U-boat after all.

The Battle of the Bulge raged on in Belgium, and though I didn't know it then, my brother Lewis was in the thick of it, driving a tank. He survived wounds sustained there, and earned a Purple Heart.

Wales, when I saw it in daylight, was the greenest land I had ever seen. The Welsh, though friendly, had accents impossible to understand.

A few weeks later, a group of us arrived by train in London in the middle of a midnight air raid. In the blackout, a guide walked in front with a hooded lantern, taking us to our billets. These turned out to be posh apartments in Mayfair, where the bathrooms boasted throne-like toilets and we each had our own large room. As a lowly private first class clerk typist, I spent my few months there writing citations for Awards and Decorations.

One evening, A V-II rocket fell on Hyde Park and the explosion nearly knocked me out of bed. To the sound of breaking glass, I rushed to get out in case the roof fell in, but could not open the door to the hall. I thought the bomb concussion had stuck it, but after a struggle I did get it open far enough to see the girl next door, pulling as hard to get in as I was pulling to get out. We collapsed on each other laughing, and decided it was safe to stay where we were.

Our mess hall was half a dozen blocks away, and I got there the next morning to be met with disbelief and amazement by WAACs from other billets. The rumor had already gone round that our building had been bombed flat.

One wonderful day I received my much sought after assignment to Paris. This was soon after the city had been liberated, and the sight so awed me that I couldn't say a word all the way from the airport to my new lodgings at the Hotel Napoleon Bonaparte, near the Arc de Triomphe and Champs Elysee. One night at the hotel a fire broke out and we WAACs ran out in the street in various stages of undress to be gaped at by a mass audience in the street, while French pompiers attacked the blaze with hoses and fire axes.

I wrote for and later edited an Air Transport Command (ATC) weekly, and sometimes walked over a few blocks to rue de Berri to borrow picture cuts from *Stars & Stripes*, which shared the building with the International Herald Tribune.

About the time our ATC weekly had its funds cut off, I was asked by an editor at *Stars & Stripes* if I'd like to replace their only woman staff writer, who was going home. So, it happened, and I began my happy experience with the paper, first in Paris and later in Berlin and Vienna.

On a trip to the Leipzig Trade Fair in the Russian Zone of Germany, I was late getting down to the hotel lobby on the first morning. The other correspondents had already departed by bus for the American mess and a rather furtive German in a drivers' uniform came up and offered to take me there by jeep.

Instead, he delivered me to the Russian Officers' mess, where Red Army men were breakfasting on black bread, sausages, pickles, and raw eggs broken over mashed potatoes. If my driver expected an award for bringing them a hostage, he was disappointed. They soon discovered I was a useless catch, with not a word of Russian and very few of German to my name. They must have told him to take me back where he found me, for that is what he did. This greatly amused my colleagues.

I met my fate in the person of a tall, charming British War Correspondent for the Associated Press on this trip. Though stationed in Frankfurt, he turned up in the Berlin Press Club. He had recently spent more than three years in Italian and German prisoner-of-war camps. Rommel's troops had captured him while he covered the Desert War in Egypt.

We waltzed right into a love that brought us to the altar in Frankfurt in 1946 and lasted through our golden anniversary. Our son and daughter, David and Jane, were born in Paris during our 16 years in France, where I covered fashions and wrote features for the AP.

When we moved to England in the early 60s, I continued to write features and fashion for the AP and a weekly column for the *International Herald Tribune*. I had lived abroad 26 years and traveled all over before we came to live in Texas again in 1970.

After my husband died a few years ago, I found his journal of prisoner of war years in his desk, typed it into my computer, and am still trying to find a publisher for it.

# *World War II in England*

## Penelope Dale

Early on the first Sunday of September 1939, in a church in a small village in southern England, my family heard the announcement that war had been declared. As a fifteen-year-old this alarmed me, yet I did not really grasp the significance of the declaration. We went home with the family where we were staying at that time, that is my mother, younger brother Neil, and I, for my father was already a Commander in the British Navy.

When we got home we got out our gas-masks, put them on and walked around to learn to breath normally as we anticipated that we might easily have to wear them much of the time. Fortunately, this never happened, and it was the first and the last time that we ever put them on.

Later that same month, I went back to the dormitory of St. Margaret's Bushey in north London where I entered the sixth form (11th grade equivalent) for my last two years of high school. From those two years, I have a number of very clear memories. I loved to play netball, lacrosse, tennis and many other sports. We could only play outside if the sirens were on "all clear."

During those two years, much of the time we found ourselves in the midst of an exciting game when the warning sirens would start wailing and we would have to run to the air raid shelters as quickly as possible. Imagine a game of tennis where you have gotten to 40-30 and you have to stop and run to the air raid shelter. The "all clear" goes and you run back to the tennis courts only to serve once, at 40-30, it is duce and the sirens go again! Not a very satisfactory way to play a tennis match.

At one point in these two years, we had all our classes in the air raid shelters, and slept there at night. We spent so much time in those shelters that finally our headmistress gave orders that when the all clears sounded, whatever we were doing we were to stop and run out on to the playing fields to get a breath of fresh air and a little exercise. Sometimes the last students hadn't left the shelter before the warning sirens sounded again and we would hastily return to our underground living quarters. I wrote many of my final exams down in these shelters.

During those two years in sixth form, I was privileged to have an interview at St. Bartholomew's hospital in the heart of the city of London. At seventeen, I secured acceptance to nursing school, but had to wait until I was eighteen-and-a-half before I could start at the Preliminary Training School. I would love to have stayed an extra year at St. Margaret's for I would have been Head Girl, captain of the lacrosse team and had various other prestigious positions. Unfortunately, my parents were very poor and they did not feel comfortable to ask the lady who had been paying for me to be at this good school, to continue to pay. So I had to leave St. Margaret's and faced what today we call a "gap year."

During my gap year, I worked at the local women's

institute. We picked fruit, such as blackberries, from the hedges around the countryside. We cooked them, and made jams, jelly or bottled the whole fruit. I also knitted socks for sailors. I always enjoyed knitting especially since my Dad was in the Navy. Although busy most of the time, I counted the days until I could start at the hospital in London.

Since I was a little girl, I had dreamed of being a nurse. I grew ever more impatient with having to wait and hang around, as I called it, when nurses were so desperately needed during those war years. But, the time finally passed and in September 1942 I started at Barts Preliminary Training School (PTS). Thankfully, our location north of London wasn't troubled with the bombing during that time. After two months, I passed the PTS exams and our whole "September 42 Set," as we were called, moved a short distance to Hill End, St. Albans. Here we started to work on the wards.

From the beginning, I loved working with the patients. Although I never excelled in the written exams, I managed to pass them with reasonable marks. I always did very well on the practical level so that by December of 1945 I was a fully qualified State Registered Nurse, (SRN).

Within six months of transferring to Hill End, the Lord sent me my future life partner. Donald, a medical student at Barts in London, had come to Cambridge University to escape the bombing. Having finished his pre-medical exams, he came to Hill End to start his time in the hospital wards. We met in the Christian Union within days of his arrival. Our hearts grew ever closer to the Lord and closer to each other.

I finished my training at the end of 1945, and Donald finished in very early May 1946. We were married at St. Martins-in-the-fields on May 10th, having fulfilled our promise to my parents that we would not get married until we had both finished our training.

During those years of training all medical students and nurses had to take their turn at the main hospital in London. At times, bombs rained down almost continuously. First came the V-1's and later the V-2's that targeted certain buildings or areas of London. I remember most vividly the V-2 that hit the crowded Smithfield market early one morning. The V-2 went through the road surface and exploded in the underground market at the busiest time of day. Barts Hospital is located very close to Smithfield market and within an hour every ward in the hospital had been opened. We admitted more than 600 patients.

Both Donald and I were in the London section of Barts at the time. Most of us worked non-stop for the next 48 hours, no time to sleep and only eating on the run. Because most patients were already evacuated to Hill End, many of our wards were closed but ready for any possible emergency. This was the only time, as far as I remember, that every ward was opened and filled within a very few hours. Those in the operating rooms worked non-stop for days. All volunteers, retired doctors, nurses, and those in other fields were called up. The challenge of this emergency showed the efficiency and I want to say, brilliance, of the British to cope with such a devastating situation.

I will always treasure these memories of the war in England.

# *A Penny Postcard*

## Carin Eagleston

I nodded solemnly. I was six years old and had just gotten my first job working on a farm. Mom Maloney and I calmly eyed the chicken as the poor headless thing continued to flop around the yard. "Keep an eye on it and let me know when it stops flopping around," she told me.

Smoothing her apron, she returned to the house, leaving me in charge. Not ten minutes before I had watched her step down off the porch and move toward the flock of chickens. Nearing them she bent down quickly, grabbed a chicken by its legs, and deftly swung the clucking, squawking bird over on its side onto a log, and, with a flick of her wrist, she swung the axe and cut off its head! It had all happened so quickly that she finished before I could blink. That was my introduction to farm life and the woman with whom I spent my next three years.

That was the summer of 1943. Those were bad times for the world and bad times for my young mother whom my father had deserted. He offered no support and my penniless mother needed to work full time. She really had no one to turn to care for her three young children. I was six and my brothers were three and two. Some of her friends helped with food and baby-sitting, but she knew that the situation couldn't continue. In desperation, she ran an ad in a newspaper looking for a home in which to board her children.

Some time later, she received several handwritten responses. I remember sitting close to my mother on a couch as she read the letters. She read each one aloud and we discussed what was and wasn't said. With the reading of each letter, I could sense my mother's unhappiness. Then, resting in her lap in the midst of all the opened envelopes was the last response–a penny postcard. She read it aloud once and read it once again. I could see that, maybe, this one sounded good to my mother. It was from a woman named Mrs. Maloney. She wrote about her farm, which she described as small, but one that had pigs and a cow and chicken—such unbelievable news for a city girl!

"Well, what do you think about this Mrs. Maloney and her farm?" questioned my mother.

I nodded and told her that I thought it was good but deep inside, I realized that I might have to leave my mother. Financial worries forced my mother to act quickly. We made the all-important decision to go to the Maloney farm.

Some days later, my mother and I and my younger brothers left our small apartment in New York City and traveled by train to the farm in New Jersey. Mrs. Maloney and her grown daughter, Ella, were waiting at the station when we stepped down from the train on that Sunday afternoon. Mrs. Maloney was a tall woman with kindly eyes and a quiet, serious manner. She calmly offered her hand to me and when I placed my hand in hers, I felt safe after feeling unsafe and uncertain for so long.

I determined Mrs. Maloney was pretty old. After all, I

could see that her daughter was about my mother's age. Ella had warm hugs for us children and a ready laugh. I learned that Ella and her husband lived in an apartment in town where she taught first grade. Mr. Maloney had waited at home. Ella explained that his eyesight was failing and he had difficulty walking. I soon discovered that his infirmities meant that the burden of maintaining the farm fell on Mrs. Maloney's shoulders. The Maloneys also had a son Frank in the army serving overseas. The war had touched everyone's lives.

With little fanfare, the Maloneys made us part of the family right from the start. It was decided then that the Maloneys would be Mom and Pop to us. This created a semblance of family and made it easier on all of us. If my mother prayed that night on the train returning to the city that her children were going to be well cared for in a loving and safe home, her prayers had been answered triple fold. No more angry words. No more tears, gone were the days and nights of anxiety for all of us. No more sudden emptying of closets and hurriedly moving clothing and children down a hall to another apartment; no more shuffling between babysitters.

The Maloney farmhouse had two-stories and living accommodations quite different from our previous experiences. It had no indoor plumbing; just an outhouse and water for the house came from a pump on a wall on the side of the house. Many times a day they drew water from the well and heated it on a large black cast iron stove. We really enjoyed bath time. The least dirty child bathed first in a large galvanized tub sitting in the kitchen; the dirtiest, last.

We spent our days playing outdoors in the cornfields near the house in the glorious sunshine. We soon turned tanned and rosy. Joy bubbled in us as we played in summer showers.

Drenched from head to toe with rain, we city children were exhausted from laughing. We had great fun collecting chicken eggs, climbing apple trees, and watching the farm animals. Sunday church and evening prayers with Pop Maloney played an important part in our lives. I started first grade in the small school up the road that September. My life couldn't have been more perfect. Life with the Maloneys moved at a graceful pace and my brothers and I lived in harmony with the world.

Sadly, I found that graceful pace changed one afternoon when I returned from school. Instead of finding Mom Maloney in the kitchen, Ella was waiting for me. I could tell she had been crying. She told me that her brother, Frank, had been killed in the battle at Normandy Beach. She wept and I wept too to see the tears on Ella's face. She hugged me and I hugged her back.

To see Ella so sad was more than my heart could bear. I promised to be a good girl and be helpful with my brothers. Ella refused offers by my mother to take us back home to the city. Ella wanted us to stay with mother especially now. Now it was our turn to be a comfort and a distraction at this sad time in Mom Maloney's life and so we stayed with them. Mom Maloney continued to go about her farm work and care for us, but, sadly, she no longer hummed her Irish tunes. The house was very, very quiet during that time.

Although my mother now worked full time, she managed to remain an active presence in our lives and we looked forward to her visits. However, during those sad weeks after Frank's death, my mother suddenly stopped coming on Sunday afternoons. She was gone a very long time and I didn't know what happened to her. At first, I was bewildered but as time went by, I felt my heart grow smaller and smaller and sadder and sadder. I was sure that my mother, too, had died. I figured that Mom Maloney and Ella felt if they didn't say anything, then I wouldn't notice. However, I did notice and I spent my days silently grieving. I didn't want to go to school any more.

Apparently, telltale signs of my grief began to emerge. I don't know exactly how they discovered my sad little secret but Ella and I had one of our talks and I confessed that I knew there was something wrong. I knew that my mother was dead just like Frank. She assured me that certainly was not the case. I later found out that mother had gone to Reno to divorce my father and had to remain there for several weeks. After Ella's talk with me, Mom Maloney began to write letters to my mother while I stood by her side and dictated my news to her in those letters. The exchange of letters reassured me that all was fine with my world again.

I stayed with the Maloneys until I was nine years old and then returned with my brothers to live once again with my mother. I would visit them sometimes and send occasional letters to keep them up to date with the milestones in my life, my wedding and my daughter's arrival. I'm grateful that their legacy of strength, courage, and compassion became a large part of who I am today.

# Big Bands and My Day to Swing and Sway with Sammy Kaye

## Col (Ret.) Max B. Scheider

My memento, an autographed baton, serves as a reminder that difficult times can have good aspects. World War II, with all of its horrors and deprivations, also provided some lighter, enjoyable opportunities.

One I remember that no longer exists, was the series of War Bond rallies held in my hometown in Ohio. I bought 25-cent stamps at my grade school and gradually accumulated enough to buy a $25 War Bond for $18.75.

However, I did not attend the War Bond rallies because of any interest in the bonds. In fact, I don't really remember much about what the speakers said about the importance of buying bonds to support the war effort.

The big attractions were the celebrities and, especially, the big bands that performed to attract the audiences. And, these attractions were free! I tried to never miss one. This introduction to the big bands began my lifelong love of that style of music.

They blocked off the street in the middle of downtown, where two of the major movie theaters stood. There they erected a huge stage for the performers, the big bands, the band singers, and the local dignitaries. They held the rallies in the summer on Friday afternoons. Coincidentally, the bands performed that weekend at the local Paramount theater.

One of the first bands that appeared there was Ozzie Nelson's. He had a girl singer named Harriet Hilliard. My children probably have no idea that this is how the stars of "Ozzie and Harriet" made their start in show business. I am also sure that my grandchildren have no idea that such a show even existed.

Among others, Gene Krupa, Cab Calloway, Benny Goodman, Count Basie, Ted Lewis, and Les Brown all performed on that stage.

I always took an early enough bus to be there in time to be leaning against the stage when the performers arrived.

I am not sure if we used the term "cool" in those days, but the singer with the band fit that description perfectly. He always had a deep voice, a fancy suit, and seemed to "have it all."

The girl singers wore evening dresses and were the most glamorous creatures that an adolescent ever saw. When not featured in a song, they stood off to the side of the band moving rhythmically with the music.

My town did not have a subway system, but I soon learned about taking the "A Train." I had not yet been to New Jersey, but I knew about the "Jersey Bounce." The war inspired many songs about separated lovers. "I'll Be Seeing You" was a reoccurring theme. I had not been in love, but I knew that it was wonderful, it was sad, and it was the major subject of the great songs.

I enjoyed my second summer with the big bands even more. I now had my first "real" job as an usher at a movie theater on the very street where they held the rallies. Along with the job came enough money to afford to pay to see the bands perform again at the Paramount after the rally.

The bands put on a real stage show between the showings of the current movie. The most exciting moments came when the movie ended and the large curtain lowered to hide the stage. The band would then start playing its theme song behind the curtain. Of course, everyone knew that song best, and the moment was magical.

One of the stage shows I paid to attend featured Sammy Kaye. During the show, he always invited four audience members to compete in a contest called "So you want to lead a band?"

When that time came, I got up enough nerve to raise my hand. Surprisingly, I was among the four he chose. I climbed the stairs to the stage and experienced the excitement of standing on the other side of the footlights.

He briefly instructed us in the art of conducting and then, in turn, he interviewed us, gave us an autographed baton, and put us in front of the band to see what we could do. I went last, so I had enough of my nerve back to actually talk and also lead "Mr. Five By Five." Afterward, to my amazement, the audience selected me, the only teenager, as the winner. I left the theater with my baton in hand, and walking on air.

Now, sixty years later, I enjoy almost all types of music. However, I still have a special fondness for those great songs from the 40s. On Sunday afternoons, I like to listen to a radio station that features the Big Bands. Amazingly, my wife and I still remember the words to most of the songs. Sometimes we just listen, and sometimes we sing along. We especially enjoyed swing dancing to the old tunes. Then we can fully appreciate the music while reminding ourselves that difficult times definitely have good aspects.

# Letter of Gratitude to My Cousin Charlie

## Dora T. Frost

Dear Charlie,

You were twelve years old when I was born and you nicknamed me "Sweet Pea." You said I looked like Popeye's baby because I was bald.

During the summers, when I spent nights at Grandpa and Grandma's house, I remember you would come to have lunch with them when you worked at the gas station nearby. I would hear your footsteps coming through the house and you would call out to me, "Sweet Pea!" You'd pick me up and carry me into the kitchen where Grandma would have lunch and a cup of coffee waiting for you.

I remember how you would tease your Mom, telling her, "Grandma isn't stingy with *her* coffee like you are!" Your Mom didn't like you to drink coffee because she said it would stunt your growth.

I remember that you were very handsome and everybody loved you. You were six feet tall, with red hair (your buddies all called you "Red"), and you were the captain of the football team. When you graduated from High School, your classmates voted you "Most Likely to Succeed."

Charlie, you dreamed of becoming a doctor and you had just started college when World War II broke out. Rather than wait for the draft, you joined the Navy in 1942. You transferred to the Marines shortly thereafter. I remember the day that the family learned of your death on September 22, 1944. Everyone cried. I was seven years old and I knew that something was terribly wrong, but I didn't understand what. I never got to say good-bye.

First hand accounts of your last days in combat written by your commanding officer, said that you had the chance to leave the company and work in sickbay, but you chose to stay in the company where you had close contact with the men in your unit. You were a good corpsman, with a sense of duty in doing your best for the Marines in your company. You worked in the thick of battle that day. You were tired and hungry, with torn dungarees, but unhurt. Casualties were heavy, but Bloody Nose Ridge had to be taken. Though close to death, you remained your usual optimistic, cheerful self as you treated the wounded.

When one Marine was killed and two others seriously wounded while attempting to evacuate casualties, you proceeded without hesitation to go to the aid of your helpless comrades. Courageously advancing alone under machine gun fire, you succeeded in treating and carrying back, unaided, four of the wounded men before you were fatally struck down.

In a letter to your parents, your commanding officer wrote, "True, your son's body is dead, but his soul lives on. His actions are forever imprinted on the minds of every living man of L Company—they remember with reverent pride. The men whose lives your son saved remember him with a soul-filling thankfulness experienced only by those who have faced death. I will forever remember him as a man, full and mature, one who showed no fear; one who was selfless in his thoughts and actions; one who put the abolition of pain and the saving of lives far above his own. Your son, Red, lives as an inspiration to all who knew him."

You were only 20 years old when you died, and you were awarded the Navy Cross (posthumously).

Charlie, you were always a hero to me, and your loss deeply affected everyone in the family. In a very real sense, the prophecy that you would be the "Most Likely to Succeed" came true. You will never be forgotten by the men whose lives you saved, or by those of us who knew you and loved you.

Good-bye, Charlie
I love you.
Sweet Pea

# *My Love*

## Ken Braselton

The first time I saw her I fell in love
She looked like an angel from above
Her shape was graceful, this gorgeous dame
I was drawn to her like a moth to a flame
Her lines were sleek, her body slim
I could tell by looking she was full of vim
I came to her with outstretched arms
Overwhelmed by her beauty and charms
She responded to me, to my every whim
Compared to others she was a priceless gem
Seduced by her presence, I was lost in my dreams
I began to envision impossible schemes
We left the earth far below
As we soared 'midst the clouds of snow
Earthly things were lost forever
We were alone, just we two, together.
Though now we are both old and dated
My love for that B-17 has never faded
That Flying Fortress, the queen of them all
Her picture still hangs on my office wall.

# A Childhood Lost in
# World War II Germany

## Rosemarie Mueller

For us children, this was one of those exciting days during World War II: Hitler had decided to enforce a "gas mask requirement" for some areas in Germany. Now all people in and around Koenigsberg/East Prussia had to keep their gas masks ready to wear at all times—dangling around their necks during daytime and within easy reach during the night.

This was the fall of 1944. I was a five-year old girl, ready for some change in our daily wartime routine. We had kept gas masks on a kitchen shelf for some time. They were of great interest to us kids, but the adults, which mostly meant our mothers, had not explained their purpose to us.

Now we learned how to use them. Not only were we willing to wear gas masks around our necks, but we eagerly learned how to put them on and keep them on for at least an hour a day. They made great toys, too.

We could scare the daylights out of the grown-ups by charging out of a dark corner wearing a gas mask. What a riot! Gas masks added a lot of excitement and fun to our games.

We did not grasp the horrible meaning of wearing gas masks every day, but it must have broken our mothers' hearts watching us running around happily while facing the threat of a poison-gas attack.

Our wartime life, the only life we younger children knew, was pretty exciting anyhow. Because of the continuous air raids, all four families of our apartment building moved down to the basement. Usually one basement room in residential buildings had reinforced beams and served as shelter during air raids. This is where we lived now. Mattresses for sleeping covered almost the entire floor of the shelter. My little brother, 18-months old, was the youngest, and our neighbors, a retired couple in their seventies, were the oldest occupants. We cooked our meals, usually vegetable soup, in a big laundry kettle in the laundry room.

For the first time in our lives, we children liked going to bed. We all took our favorite toy, usually a doll or a teddy bear, and willingly marched to our sleeping corner. We loved to spend all night with our friends. I don't think the grown-ups expected us to go to sleep right away, but we had to be quiet while our mothers listened to the BBC, an English radio station that broadcast news in German about wartime Germany.

Of course, I did not comprehend anything they talked about, and secrecy surrounded everything about BBC broadcasts. We kids had promised, by everything we cherished, that we would not let anybody know that our mothers listened to the enemy station. I learned later that this was the only way for Germans to obtain accurate information. But getting caught listening to the BBC also meant severe punishment, even the death penalty. Our neighbors, relatives, and friends were not informers who would betray us to the authorities. However, Hitler's secret service, the Gestapo, would threaten people with harm to their families to extort this information.

The noise of the bombs crashing into nearby buildings, the cries of the injured, and the moans of the dying frightened us children. However, when an attack ended, most of the time we would continue to play, eat, and sleep. Our lives were not consumed by our mothers' fears of the next attack, of dying, of losing our loved ones, of running out of food and shelter. Our mothers surely thought of nothing else. Only many years later, when I was a mother myself, could I truly comprehend the extent of their suffering.

When it got dark in the evening and our mothers thought it safe to venture outside, we went to our adjacent garden and dug a deep, wide hole to bury some food such as root vegetables, canned fruit, and dry goods. We also packed clothes and blankets in boxes and hid them there. At that time, everything, especially food, was extremely scarce. I think our mothers feared that even harder times were ahead. We children loved to help dig the holes with our little shovels and carrying boxes and cans to bury there. As with the radio listening, we kept this secret. Withholding food from the German military and civilian population was considered a crime of betraying the Fuehrer and endangering the war effort.

By early January 1945, bombs and fires had destroyed much of our neighborhood. The deaths of so many neighbors and friends, the mounting heaps of rubble around us, and the news from BBC London convinced my mother to leave Koenigsberg. The enemy badly wanted to capture this city, because it has the only year-round ice-free harbor to the

Baltic Sea. My mother probably hoped that moving further west, away from the Red Army, would provide a better chance of survival.

At night, while bombs fell continuously, we walked to the train station. For a week, we tried to catch a train leaving Koenigsberg, but with a toddler and a small child, chances were slim. Continuous air raids on the trains and train stations made boarding trains during daytime impossible. At night, crowds of desperate mothers tried to board the trains or throw their youngsters through train windows into the compartments in the hope that someone would catch them and care for them. My mother could not bring herself to do this. We finally went back to our basement shelter in Koenigsberg.

A few weeks later, probably in early February 1945, my mother stuffed our backpacks with food and clothes and put my little brother in his stroller together with some diapers, my doll, and his teddy bear. At night, a neighbor with a horse-drawn cart brought us to the harbor. We caught a freight boat to Rauschen, a small vacation town at East Prussia's Samland Coast, an area not as heavily bombed as Koenigsberg. However, the boats, moving slowly near the coastline toward Rauschen, made easy targets and Russian planes bombed and strafed them continuously. Stiff with fear and cold, we cowered on deck watching bombs drop onto boats and into the water. Many mothers and children drowned when their boats exploded and sank. In my nightmares, I still hear their screams. I will probably hear them to the end of my life.

Luckily, our boat made it to Rauschen. We moved into a deserted house by the coast with many other women and children we did not know.

Most days, the adults left early in the morning to search for food. They went to deserted houses, stores, and farms but they never found enough of anything. Many Germans believed until the end that Hitler would win the war and save us. However, my mother thought our situation was hopeless and that we would not survive the war.

When Mother went scavenging, I cared for my little brother as best as I could, giving him water when he cried and changing his diapers. With only strangers in the house, we kept to ourselves. I lived in constant fear that Mother might get killed on one of her food-hunting trips and not come back. Although our mothers gave most of the food to us children, we suffered from malnutrition, diarrhea, and the horrors we had experienced.

Before our mothers left for their daily food-hunting trips, they admonished us to run for shelter to the nearby bunker during an air attack. If we were outside when low-flying planes approached, we were to lie flat on the ground, motionless. They shot at everything that moved.

Most of the time, we did not follow our mothers' instructions but stayed on our mattresses in the house. A great apathy had befallen us. Hunger and the traumatic events of the war had exhausted us. We seldom laughed or cried any more. On the boat, I had lost my doll. I didn't care. It didn't matter. Years passed before I played again.

# Mission Unknown

As told to June Venable by
lst Lt. John R. Venable Gunnery Officer,
5<sup>th</sup> Squadron, 9<sup>th</sup> Bomb Group

The Island of Tinian, located in the northern end of the Marianas, had the largest airfield in the world in 1945. To the south of Tinian sits the well-known and densely populated island of Guam, which at that time contained the Headquarters for the 20<sup>th</sup> Air Force.

Very few people knew about Tinian, therefore it was missed by News Correspondents, USO Troops and Bob Hope. To keep up morale, some enterprising soul came up with "Club Tinian."

The Club, a radio broadcast, originated from beautiful Tinian surrounded by the blue Pacific Ocean. They played dance music, ice tinkling in glasses, and voices of people (including females), all having a wonderful time. A voice came in occasionally to describe the scene, making most of us wish we were there. However, we soon discovered that the Club was nothing more than the invention of an enterprising amateur DJ, broadcasting from a closet only large enough to hold his equipment.

The south end of the island contained a harbor, and boats of various kinds regularly came in and out. Those on the boats could hear the broadcasts and once ashore, many immediately started looking for the entertainment. There were no signs, nor transportation, but directions were "graciously" given to "Club Tinian."

In late July of 1945, as several of us were having an idle-moment discussion, it occurred to us that we had never seen an order, a memorandum, or directive saying we couldn't visit the 509th Composite Group area. Everything about the secrecy on this project came by word-of-mouth.

Four of us decided to drive over to see what was going on. The minute we drove into the area, four marines standing around an airplane of the 6th and 9th Bomb Groups, took their carbines off their shoulders and looked directly at us. We did a U-turn, never spoke of it or went back again.

On the afternoon of August 6, 1945, at North Field, several people were relaxing in the shade of an airplane wing. The calmness seemed a bit strange and we wondered about it. Suddenly, an excited individual ran up and disclosed that a B-29 from the 509th had just landed and General Spaatz and several other Generals were handing out medals to the crew. The General's name rang bells immediately. He was the commander of the entire air war in the Pacific, and General Curtis LeMay's boss. We knew something big was going on, but the lethargic group lying in the shade, didn't move. No one was curious enough to learn the reason for the ceremony.

The next morning at breakfast, an 8-1/2 x 11 mimeographed sheet of paper was available for those who cared to read it. The headlines were: ATOM BOMB DROPPED ON JAPAN. A brief description of the Enola Gay followed. This was the off-limits airplane we weren't allowed to see.

Still there was no cheering, no loud conversation, nothing to indicate that we knew the meaning of those headlines. It was the first news that most of us had as to what had happened the previous day. That meant that we were some of the last in the world to know the impact of the Enola Gay's mission, which was the beginning of the end of World War II.

# Our Garden

## Ann Holden

My parents loved being outdoors, or more accurately, they needed it for their mental health. Their outdoor togetherness started early in their relationship when they met at a bird-watching club. They seemed fated to embrace the outdoor life.

Although my father was intelligent, he had to quit school in the seventh grade to help his widowed mother support the family. He could only do blue-collar jobs so not only did he have to work inside, he was in a dark, windowless, noisy factory that lacked all he loved: fresh air, sunshine, birds, and the chance to enjoy nature in silence.

My mother finished high school and had a love of learning. The Depression had hurt her family and with five children supported by a house painter, college wasn't possible for any of them. That led my mother to work in an office. Neither of my parents complained to us children but we knew they missed being outside.

In 1951, our landlord in Madison raised the rent to the outrageous sum of $35 per month. My parents decided to look for a place to buy, preferably in the country. They bought a recently closed one-room schoolhouse outside of Cottage Grove, Wisconsin, plus some adjacent land for a total of about five acres. The combination of circumstances: available land, love of the outdoors and a scarcity of cash, led us naturally to planting a large garden.

Strawberries were the first crop of spring. They were tender, red and juicy. When preparing them, we gently pulled on the stem and it came out naturally. They were so soft that the knife slid through silently. Some modern strawberries are so firm they sound like an apple being sliced.

My father told people at work that he had strawberries for sale and they drove out to buy them. One time I was selecting some for one of his co-workers because my parents weren't home. I assumed we would only sell the best and I was a harsh critic. If I judged them too soft, or they had some blemish that made them less than perfect, I just threw them over my shoulder into the garden. The man didn't say anything at the time but he later told my dad that I had thrown away what looked to him like perfectly good berries.

Our favorite dessert was Strawberry Shortcake. My mother and I made the shortcake from scratch. We would have none of the sponge cakes currently on the market. We didn't smother it with whipped cream, fresh or from an aerosol can. We just added a little sugar to bring out the flavor.

The non-commercial harvest included green beans, Swiss chard, radishes and wonderfully tender green beans. We had so many, even though we wasted very little of anything, we would eat only the young, tender beans. We were as selective in choosing beans as we were with strawberries. If they got big enough to have lumpy beans inside, we rejected them.

The radishes were fun. They grew so fast it seemed they

sprouted out of the ground in a matter of days, and were ready to eat in a couple of weeks. The small ones were good but they got bitter with age so once I dared my younger brother to eat a very large one. He got it down but his eyes watered. He has probably long since forgotten about it but I still feel guilty.

My brothers and I came up with a combination I never heard of before or since, but we regularly had peanut butter and radish sandwiches. I know that most people put sweet stuff with peanut butter, but we would thinly slice a radish or two and put some slices on a peanut butter sandwich. The slightly sharp, tangy flavor went well with peanuts. The combination of crisp and creamy textures plus the red and white slices on brown peanut butter appealed to us. It has not caught on as a culinary delight, and I doubt a trend will start by those that read about it here.

We grew many bushels of cucumbers and sold them to a pickle factory. Cucumber vines creep along the ground, never getting more than a few inches tall. Picking "cukes," as we called them, presents a challenge because they hide under the broad, rough leaves and as they got big, would lie right on the ground. We did a lot of bending over to pick them. My father used salty, picturesque language when he wanted us to stick to our task of picking. He'd yell, "All I want to see are asses and elbows." We kept on picking.

We also grew fresh dill. My mother made the best dill pickles ever. She stuffed cucumbers and dill into sterilized jars, filled them with brine, and a few months later we had world-class pickles. They were so good that whenever my mother went to a potluck supper people asked her to bring pickles, that was all, just a jar of pickles.

Nature saved the best for last; tomatoes and sweet corn.

In August, we ate fresh tomatoes until we got sores in our mouths, then sold or canned the rest. I remember growing a variety called Beefsteak, just as luscious as the name implies. They were juicy, plump with pulp, and felt heavy in your hand. They were not the pink vinyl with skin and seeds that some growers call tomatoes.

I loved to help with the canning. We would put a huge pan full of tomatoes between us, pour hot water over them so the skins would slip off easily, and then cut them into quarters. I loved the feel of the slippery vegetable and all the juice dripping between my fingers. My mother would use a big pressure cooker to process the filled jars. It scared me because I thought it would blow up. It never did but I still don't cook with a pressure cooker.

Sweet corn was another abundant crop. You can't grow just a little bit of it. You must plant several rows so it will pollinate. When we walked down the rows to pick the corn, the leaves felt rough on our arms. Corn grows taller than an average adult and rumor has it that corn grows so fast that under the right conditions you can hear it grow at night, a great bit of folklore even if it's not precisely true.

We believed that corn should be knee-high by the 4$^{th}$ of July and ripen by early August. Every year the little town of Sun Prairie has a Sweet Corn Festival, one of the cultural, gustatory, and free events of Dane County. I remember eating two ears of steamed-in-the-husk corn. The men serving pulled back the hot husks, wiped out the silk and using a paintbrush slathered it with melted butter. That's gourmet eating!

We sold some of our abundant corn crop door-to-door in the city, asking only a dollar for a dozen ears. We knew about the importance of freshness when picking and cooking corn. My father used to tell us to put the water on to boil, then go pick the corn. It was rare to get it that fresh. Once we offered it to a gentleman who asked when we picked it. When our reply was, that morning, to our surprise he said it was too old, perhaps all of five hours by that time. He must have used the same guidelines as my father.

Wisconsin soil is very fertile. A geologist friend says it's the product of glacial grinding. Facts aside, my father claimed that the soil was so good you could plant a shingle and grow a roof. We never fertilized or watered anything. I doubt that we sprayed for bugs for fear that it was bad for the birds that my parents so loved. We were organic before it was called organic.

Living in the country, made gardening an important part of our family life and the education of my brothers and me. It taught us agronomy, economics, nutrition, exercise physiology, and at least a little theology. I'm glad I had a childhood filled with these lessons.

# *Finding my True Love – November 1951*

## Donna Van Straten Remmert

Kathy Vanden Heuval and I sat next to each other in a school assembly today and instead of listening to teachers preach about school rules, we whispered about our love lives. Actually, Kathy did most of the talking because she knows everything about it since she's a junior and is going steady. We're friends and she doesn't even care that I'm just a freshman. Anyway, something she said today has really got me thinking.

"Lots of girls find a man to marry in their freshmen year," she said.

"Holy jeepers," I said back. "How can that possibly happen? First semester is already half over and I've had only one date so far!"

"Well, I'm going to marry the first guy I ever dated," Kathy said. "It happens a lot."

She told me all about her first date and it was the most romantic story I've ever heard. It was with Horse Klarner when she was a freshman. I guess he's already proposed because she talks like she knows they'll get married.

"Everyone calls him Horse but me," she explained. "I call

him Larry because I don't like saying Horse when I'm whispering sweet nothings into his ear."

Wow, whispering sweet nothings sounds like in the movies but it's Kathy's honest-to-goodness real life. I can tell that she's in love with Horse from the way she says things.

My first date was with Terry Kuehne. He's a real hunk and I'd marry him except for one thing, he's not Catholic.

"It'll happen when it happens," Kathy said, "and from then on you'll be on Cloud Nine."

"Really? Tell me exactly how it could happen, okay?" I got so excited to hear more that my whispers became too loud.

Coach Wolk came over to our aisle and glared at us. So Kathy pretended she was taking notes about school rules, but what she was really doing was writing me this note: *You meet your Prince Charming when you're a freshman, you start going steady when you're a sophomore, he gives you his class ring when you're a junior, and then you get married the summer you graduate.*

"Gosh," I whispered as softly as possible, "it's amazing to think that I might be someone's wife just three years from now."

It sounded like a good thing when I was talking to Kathy, but now I'm not so sure, because I don't know enough about being someone's wife. Okay, what I do know is that after you're married, it's not a sin to go all the way anymore. That's what you do on your honeymoon. What I don't know is exactly how doing "it" is done.

Wow, just the thought of it makes me tingle, like when I got kissed for the first time. I'd feel horrible if I didn't make my husband happy because of doing something wrong on our honeymoon. It's supposed to be a perfect time so I'd like to find out about this stuff before I go on mine.

We read a chapter about being a good wife in our home economics textbook but it didn't say anything about doing "it." It told us how to be a good wife in other ways and to be honest. "It" doesn't sound that easy. For instance, before a husband comes home from work everyday, a good wife has to do so many things. She has to make sure the house is neat and tidy, make sure that she and the children are clean and dressed in freshly ironed clothes, and make sure that a good dinner is ready and waiting but not burned. That's a lot to pay attention to at the last minute so it's no wonder mama gets all fidgety just before daddy comes home from work.

The book also said that a wife should tell her husband happy stories about her day rather than complaints. Otherwise, he might want to stay at work and talk to the ladies who work for him. Lots of ladies work for my dad at the sauerkraut factory and I've even seen them flirt with him. I don't think mama worries that daddy will like them better because they aren't at all good looking in those ugly plastic bonnets they have to wear when they're canning kraut. It's a government rule.

Mama sometimes tells daddy happy stories but just last week she out-and-out complained about him not appreciating how hard she works all day. "I shop for the groceries, I cook the meals, I clean the house, I wash and iron the clothes, all the while tending to the baby and keeping track of two girls in high school and three girls in grade school. If you think that's such a picnic you ought to try it for just one day!"

Gosh, when I listened to her tell about it, it really made me wonder. And, she didn't even mention that my big brother Jimmy sends his dirty clothes to her every week. She washes and irons them before she sends them back to his dormitory at college. She bakes a batch or two of cookies to put in the box. Being a good wife is hard!

Another thing to think about is that not all girls find a man to marry. I asked about this when we were discussing the good-wife chapter in home economics. "What if I never get married?" I asked. "Then I won't have to be a wife." Everyone laughed but it's not so far-fetched, is it? There are two old maids in little ol' Black Creek, Wisconsin so just think how many there are in the whole United States.

"Yes, of course," Mrs. Patchett said. "Some women never find the right man to marry and this is why it's important to take typing and shorthand while in high school. You may need to provide a living for yourself." Mrs Patchett also mentioned going to college to become a teacher, a nurse or something else that's suitable.

Kids always say that I'm pretty gutsy so who knows, I might go to college someday. Not many girls do but you never know, I might. Daddy says there are communists at Wisconsin colleges but I think Senator Joe McCarthy will get rid of them before I've graduated high school and save up enough money.

It was fun hearing Kathy tell about her future but maybe it's silly to think about mine when it's so far away. And what the heck, I'm already on Cloud Nine, ever since Terry Kuehne said that he wants to take me home from tonight's sock hop. I wonder if he's my one and only true love? Maybe after tonight I'll know.

# Lyndon and Lingerie

## Mary Gordon Spence

I remember my first day of almost everything, but none quite so clearly as my first day on the job working for former president Lyndon B. Johnson. I still remember how cute I felt dressed in a very short, black and white skirt with a white high collar blouse, complete with white hose and black patent leather shoes, and a full slip. Well, not exactly full, but like the skirt, it was at least four inches above my knees, and it made the slightly sheer blouse respectable.

As I pressed the elevator button, I knew that only a select group of people could go to the ninth floor of the Federal Building. The doors opened and I entered an already crowded elevator. By the time I reached the seventh floor, however, I was the only rider, so I did what any self-respecting woman who wanted to make a good impression would do: I hiked up my skirt and pulled down my blouse, making sure it was properly tucked in.

I untwisted the elastic waistband on my nylon hose and adjusted the straps on my slip. Then I spit on my patent leather shoes and shined them with the palm of my hand. At the last minute, I swiped a finger across my front teeth to remove any traces of lipstick that might mar my smile.

Then the elevator stopped right on cue on the ninth floor. The door opened, and I stepped out into a brave new world. Three men with guns stood beside the elevator as I emerged.

"May we help you?" one of them asked.

"Yes, I'm Mary Gordon Spence, and I'm here to work for President Johnson."

"We know who you are, Miss Spence. And we have just seen your underwear."

"My underwear?"

"Yes, ma'am. The first thing you gotta learn around here, little lady, is that there are hidden cameras everywhere."

It took me two months to work up my courage to go to the bathroom on that job. No matter how many times the Secret Service Agents tried to convince me that there were no cameras in the stalls, the memory of their smirking faces made me leery.

So my advice to you is when you start a new job, just go ahead and show your underwear right off.

From there, things can only get better.

# My First Car

Patricia Riggs Flathouse

When I turned fourteen I got my driver's license. This was almost fifty years ago in the Texas Panhandle town where I lived. We lived a long way from my high school and I had to ride downtown very early in the morning with my dad as he went to work. He would drop me off and then, after school, I would either walk a few blocks to my grandmother's house to wait for him to pick me up, or my mother would have to come downtown to pick me up. A third choice would have been to walk a mile or so to my dad's office and wait for him to leave in the evening. I didn't choose this option very often.

Because of this transportation arrangement, I began to hint broadly that I would be more than happy to drive myself to school if my dad would let me use his car, or if I had my own car. However, in the late 1950s not many high school students were privileged enough to have their own cars. Therefore, my hints were only a half-hearted effort.

During my junior year in high school, my grandmother had a stroke and was no longer able to drive. One afternoon she suggested that I take her car and drive home. I had never driven her 1948 Plymouth but was delighted with the offer.

I went to her garage and climbed into the seat but was a bit dismayed to discover that the rear window was about the size of my hand. However, undaunted I began to back the huge, lumbering old car down her long driveway and past her portico with its tall white columns. Suddenly I heard a big crunch and an even bigger thud. I jumped out of the car and looked around. I discovered that I had hit the steps of her porch with the back fender and dislodged one of the big white pillars that, luckily, fell onto the grass. My grandmother and her housekeeper came out onto the front porch with looks of horror on their faces. Their looks added to my own dismay at what I had done.

I called my dad and he very graciously came to my rescue. He surveyed the damage, probably muttering under his breath as he did so. He put the car back into the garage, propped the pillar back up under the portico and took me home. In the following weeks, he had the fender of the car fixed and my grandmother's porch repaired, but he never said a word to make me feel any worse about what I had done.

Eventually, the old green Plymouth made its way out to our house. Occasionally my dad would drive it to work so that I could use his car for my own transportation needs while I was in high school. I steadfastly refused to drive the old green Plymouth because I thought of crunching fenders and falling columns every time I looked at it. Because of my fear of driving that car, it often sat in the driveway at our house while I continued riding into town with my dad and having my mother pick me up after school.

When I left home for college my dad offered to let me take the Plymouth with me but I refused. I told him that I would rather walk than drive that old thing, so he said I could walk.

I was on a small campus and I felt very comfortable walking until the cold, snow, and icy Panhandle wind came along. Then I began to have second thoughts about needing a car, and the old green Plymouth didn't seem like such a bad idea after all. Finally, during the Christmas holidays, I decided to take the Plymouth out for a test drive. My dad gave me much needed instructions on the art of using the choke in that car. Much to my surprise, I found that it was a very easy car to drive as long I remembered how to manipulate the choke and was aware of the diminished view to the rear. I practiced driving it around town for a few days and decided that it wasn't such a bad car after all.

When I returned to school in January, it was with some pride at having my own set of wheels, but with a little embarrassment too, at having such a big, old car. However, no one made fun of it, so I relaxed and began to enjoy being able to drive my friends and myself around town. I remember coming out of the dorm one particularly icy, snowy day with the weather too frigid to walk across campus to the cafeteria.

Several girls went out to start their cars and it was evidently too cold for them to start. I got in my car, adjusted the choke, turned the key and the motor began to purr as usual. I loaded everyone into my car and we headed off to the cafeteria. There seemed to be no limit to the number of people I could load into the spacious innards of my car.

Somewhere along the line, I began, with great affection, to call my car "Shifty" because of its standard transmission. I had several arguments with various friends that cars usually had girl's names because they were temperamental. My argument for keeping the name "Shifty" was that my large green Plymouth was very strong and dependable like a man.

I drove my first car, Shifty, for about five years and had very little trouble with it even though I drove it back and forth across Texas several times a year while I was in college. I had put nearly 100,000 miles on that car while I had it. When I finally graduated and got a job, I was able to buy a car of my own. I then gave Shifty to my brother who was just beginning college. He drove Shifty for another five years and then, without asking anyone, traded it for an old Volkswagen which lasted him about six months. We were aggravated with him because Shifty was just about old enough to be declared an antique and it still ran very well.

I have often wondered whatever happened to Shifty, such a wonderful, dependable old friend!

# *My First Motorcycle*

## Paula Stephens-Bishop

In 1965, a magazine ad caught my attention and as I focused on the advertisement, my sound judgment and caution evaporated. Perched on a metallic-red bike, a gorgeous blonde touted her enthusiasm for fun and motorcycles. I was hooked!

Visions of myself zipping along streets and roaring into supermarket parking lots swirled through my thoughts. I knew my motorcycle would create a terrific sensation wherever I rode.

For Mother's Day, I asked for my own bike.

My husband laughed. "A motorcycle? You're a bundle of nerves when you ride behind me."

Our son, Clay, snickered. "Sounds kinda scary for pedestrians."

"Please. Spare me." Our teenage daughter snorted. "Mom, do you realize how embarrassed I'd be if people saw you?"

Persistence paid off. Friday was the magic day. My first motorcycle was glossy white, fully dressed with fiberglass saddlebags, windshield, and came complete with a helmet and instructions. The five language manual detailed simple procedures to start, shift, and stop.

After a hurried glance through the guidelines, I stepped outside. Blessed with a perfect spring day, I inhaled fresh air. The scent of lilacs and honeysuckle wafted on gentle breezes. Full of enthusiasm, I fastened my helmet, straddled the bike, and immediately flooded the carburetor.

Exasperated, I opened the manual, studies the "how to start" section, then entrusted the segment to memory.

Amazed, I discovered the bike came equipped with a small, black button. From hands-on experience, I was frustrated to learn constant use of this significant button tends to rundown the battery.

The manual referred to a kick-starter. After much effort, I compared the device to a dreaded implement of torture. An hour later, exhausted and drenched in sweat, I staggered inside.

When my husband arrived home, he kicked once, and then shook his head when the engine roared to life. "You must have read the manual's German or French version. Hop on and let's find a deserted lot. You need some lessons before you hurt someone."

I scrambled on and wrapped my arms around his waist. His takeoff speed was breathtaking. My grip tightened to a hammerlock.

After several weaving trips around the school's concreted area, my confidence was two on a scale of one to ten. Apprehensively, I managed a wobbly U-turn and returned to my starting point.

As though he were a professional, my husband sat beneath a shade tree barking directions. "All you need is practice. Give it a little gas, make a few more rounds, and when you're satisfied, rev the throttle. You'll never get a bike's feel going two miles per hour."

Over the weekend, I developed the perfect rev.

Monday I hurried the kids off to school, grabbed my helmet, and dashed outside. Eyeing my adorable bike, I inhaled a deep breath, straddled the seat, and then touched the dreaded black button. The engine hummed.

For practice, I rode around our block, around and around and around. Before long, our neighborhood was involved. Preschoolers formed a tricycle brigade. Along our route, our entourage grew to include dogs, and a couple of Moms on bicycles. The memory of our spontaneous parade lingers to this day.

By afternoon, my confidence skyrocketed. I knew my second grader would appreciate a ride home from school.

Clay's friend, Bob, spotted me first. His exclamation carried over the bike's purr. "Look! There's a crazy woman under a helmet."

My son grimaced. "Ah-hhh, don't act dumb. You recognize Mom."

Bob grinned. "Yeah, but she sure looks goofy on a bike. But, since she's your mom, she's okay."

Dashing to the motorcycle, he yelled. "Can I have a lift?"

Shaking his head, Clay cautioned. "Now who's goofy? You'd better be careful. She's dangerous."

Motioning toward the back, I grinned. "Hop on."

A month later, I met a delightful lady who shared my zeal for motorcycles. She road a red, step-through bike, and happened to be a trail rider. Nadine became more than a friend. We were bike buddies and shared extraordinary, incredible, once-in-a-lifetime experiences.

To ride the trails I needed to modify my bike. Off came

the windshield and saddlebags. Nadine and I headed for the rough. I was the captain. She was the loyal sidekick.

We rode together five days a week from nine till three. Rain, snow and dust were minor distractions. Trail riding was in our blood.

We zipped through sand, water and thickets, climbed rugged hills and rocky trails. Unaware of danger, we once plunged through a snake-infested gully. Fear streaked up and down my spine as we maneuvered out of the precarious situation. On the Canadian River, terrified, I inched through an area of quicksand.

Life is full of surprises. Unique friendships last a season or a lifetime as circumstances change. Memories of the God given relationship my sidekick and I shared are precious. I preserve each dusty ride in my treasure chest of sentimental journeys.

# *Prentending to be a Skier*

## P. Paulette MacDougal

What am I doing here on this mountaintop in winter? I hate the cold, even a little cold. I hate the snow. When we lived in Minnesota, I shoveled several lifetimes' worth of snow each winter. For seven months of the year, the snowplow driver viciously dumped his huge load of ice chunks into the mouth of our driveway, after Frank, who liked to shovel snow, left for work.

Along with the cold and the snow, I can do without two more things: speed and danger. So there must be some reason why at sixty-two, I find myself here on a mountaintop attached by heavy boots to two colorful boards. Behind me, large letters on each board spell out, "Predator." Do I look like a predator?

Clad in stylish purple ski clothes proffered by the neighborhood garage sales, I am sporting a space age purple jacket and thickly insulated snow pants. Underneath, I have three pairs of long underwear under stretchy jeans. A purple sweater, puffy purple gloves, purple goggles, a furry purple hat, and a purple neck warmer complete my outfit. Not a predator, but an over-ripe grape impaled on a pair of toothpicks.

I'm sweating but I'll never admit that. I believe in the cold. My hands will be cold, in spite of these puffy gloves. My head will get cold, well, the part that's not hidden under purple goggles or covered by my purple hat. My neck, under my purple neck warmer, will even be cold. I may be a plump, purple snow monster, but I will get cold.

Realizing that I'm sweating creates a new worry: Sweating will make me cold, especially because I'm standing still, a few yards from the lift, too scared to move. I look across the valley and I spot our house on the opposite mountain, miles away. It looks like a little white toy house among other toy houses. I want to be there snugly warm, curled up with a book, and safe. Yes, I want to be safe!

What was I thinking last summer when I went with Frank to buy a season ski pass with ten days of skiing prepaid. Summer's warmth and level ground seduced me into the illusion that I could ski. I blame this misconception on people who asked, "Do you ski?"

"Of course I ski!"

Everyone in Colorado skis! It's assumed and expected. When you spend time in Colorado near one of the best skiing mountains in the world, it's too embarrassing to say "No I don't ski." That's how I was shamed into it and why I'm up here on this mountain. Colorado's natural splendor can create a powerful force.

There seems to be only one way down, down. No doubt broken bones loom in my future. If I keep standing here, morning will turn to night and I will certainly freeze to death.

Frank says, "You go first, I'll follow."

"No, you go first and I'll follow," I respond.

He takes off. Slowly, because he's really a nice guy. I

follow, because freezing to death presents an unattractive option. I proceed carefully. I do know how to do this, right? Didn't I take a ski lesson just yesterday on the bunny hill! Which was one or two degrees above flat and didn't feel like this at all!

So I follow. I wipe out at the first dip in unfamiliar territory. I thrash in the snow and realize why Frank should ski behind me, not ahead. As I struggle to stand up, hampered by a clumsy space boot and a slick board on each foot, I discover new meaning to the term "slippery slope." Stuck in the snow, I'm discouraged. No. I'm desperate.

I know I'm cold. I'm sitting in the snow and reason tells me I'm cold. I just can't feel the cold because I'm sweating so much. Frank finally side-steps up the mountain to offer me a hand. Well, not his hand, he offers me his pole. Gripping the end of it, and after some awkward tries, I struggle back up to vertical. The bottom of the hill, which I can't see, is very far down. This is supposed to be fun?

"Okay, Frank, you ski behind me, so you can pick me up."

I hate this. If I reach the bottom in one piece, I will say, "I tried. Forget it. Good-bye."

Frank will say, "Nine more days of skiing, pre-paid. We bought you new skis, new boots, new poles. You're gonna ski."

But, I don't say these things because just as I'm brushing the snow off from my third fall, a woman in a fashionably sleek red ski outfit speeds by. Two swishes, and she's down the hill, almost out of sight. So fast she goes. But not so fast that I miss the fact she's not young. Older than me, I guess. I also notice she has only one ski. One ski! Geeze! What confidence! What Grace! What pizzazz! Another look confirms that she has only one ski because she has only one leg! If she can do that....

I start cautiously down the hill, calling up some affirmations: Anything you can conceive, you can achieve. Everything begins with the first step. Think like a skier, be a skier. Soft snow, soft fall. I am talking to myself aloud as I slowly move forward: Skiing is fun; everyone says so, otherwise why would they come all this distance and pay all this money to do it? It's the closest thing to flying, they say. If they can do this, I can do this, nothing to it. Piece of cake. I can do it I can do it....

I amaze myself: I do it. At the bottom of the mountain, I don't use my prepared speech about quitting. Instead, pretending I'm somebody else, I get back on them, ski a bit, fall down, figure out how to get up, fall down, and do it again and again.

After several days skiing on my own, I was able to stop and notice that the air smelled sweetly nonexistent. The view of other snow-capped peaks from a mountaintop is even more majestic and spectacular than from below. The Earth has a new shape from up there. The colors look different. I love looking down on clouds. And the wind on my face while I'm in motion is cold but exciting, a new sensation, as if the wind and the mountain and I have joined in a whole new dance. It didn't even feel cold. Correction: It did feel cold but a good kind of cold, like ice cream is cold, cold and delicious.

# *A Legacy*

## Judith S. Flournoy

I wish you learn not to lean on your own understanding, but come to have faith in your Maker's and seek to understand.

Try to enjoy your own company by spending time alone in silence doing nothing or something creative. Talk to yourself and to God while you're doing it. Silence and solitude help you get in touch with your inner values and give you answers.

I also wish for you the gift of joy, not happiness, but joy. There is a difference. Happiness is fleeting, but joy sustains. And, no matter how old you get, learn as much as you can, try new things and seek out change. Do this consistently and adventures will fill your life, some small some big. A multitude of blessings and gifts await you. Expect to find them and you will.

Printed in the United States
730800003B